QUICK!
I NEED TO BE A LEADER
IN 30 DAYS!
Follow Our Four Step System

BRAD DUDE
Foreword by Scott Blanchard

DUDE PUBLISHING

Secrets of Temperament (The Series)
Quick! I Need to Be a Leader in 30 Days!

QUICK!

I NEED TO BE A LEADER
IN 30 DAYS!

Follow Our Four Step System

*To my wife, Sue, and to the members
of the Quick Leadership Group!*

Table of Contents

WHAT PEOPLE ARE SAYING ABOUT THIS BOOK

"One of the easiest, truest measures of leadership is the ability to turn conflict from a divisive, adversarial source of stress and malfunction into a unifying, collaborative opportunity for creativity and organizational learning. The great value of this book is that it tells you how, and offers many quick, practical techniques in the art of leadership. Buy it and keep it handy."

—Kenneth Cloke, co-author of *Resolving Conflicts at Work: 10 Strategies for Everyone on the Job*

"It is rare that a 'how to book' has universal appeal. This book does so by the diversity of skills that Brad discusses. Serious leaders will find this book informative and a useful reference. The focused and concise presentation makes it an easy read. I recommend it to any serious manager or leader."

—Dr. Jim Colvard (former Deputy Director, Office of Personnel Management)

"Everything they forgot to teach you at school! Brad Dude's new leadership book highlights the need for understanding and mastering the basics of influence when stepping into leadership and introducing organizational change."

—Teresa de Grosbois #1 International bestselling author of *Mass Influence - the habits of the highly influential*

"Striving to teach a person to become an effective leader in 30 days really forces the author to zero in on the essentials—with no time or space to spare. In a concise and integrated manner, Brad includes a diverse assortment of vital leadership skills for today's organizational world. Whether new to the leadership arena or not, the reader will benefit from this streamlined presentation of the fundamentals of leadership practice."

—Ralph H. Kilmann, co-author of the *Thomas-Kilmann Conflict Mode Instrument* and CEO of Kilmann Diagnostics.

FOREWORD

When Brad asked me to write a foreword to his book, I was delighted for two reasons.

First, Brad was the partner and collaborator of one of my dearest friends in the world, Jim Harden. Jim and I met in graduate school 25 years ago during which time we both learned about temperament and the work of Carl Jung. Jim and I had a long and close relationship. Jim and Brad worked together to create the Basic Elements of Temperament approach that is a central component to this book. Since Jim died a few years ago, Brad has remained dedicated to spreading the knowledge and use of the Basic Elements approach and model to learning.

Second, this book is focused on helping new leaders and managers succeed in their new roles. I am interested and dedicated in helping new leaders make this transition as effectively as possible. Today, in America, there are record numbers of employees making the transition into management and leadership. Of course, many of these new leaders are members of the millennial generation. There are about 50 million millennials in the workforce in North America. About 10 million are in management positions and approximately 2 million millennials are entering management each year. These numbers are significant. The sad truth, however, is that 60 percent of managers fail to achieve success in the first year by their own personal measures and by the success measures of the organizations where they work. Even more frightening, the habits and skills a new leader or manager develops their first year tend to stay with them throughout their careers. Positive skills and habits become a strong foundation for a successful career in management and leadership. Poor or ineffective skills hobble a manager for years to come.

One last sad fact is relevant about making the transition into management. You are most likely going to make this transition alone. Yes, most managers do not receive training on how to manage until they have been in management for an average of 7-9 years. I am here to say you cannot depend on the organization you work with to provide the skills and knowledge you will need to succeed as a manager or leader.

Quick! I Need to Be a Leader in 30 Days! is appropriately titled because the transition to manager happens quickly and yet the people you work with, the new direct reports, will expect you have the skills, knowledge and experience to manage them fairly and skillfully. Your direct reports also may not be willing to extend you the benefit of the doubt as you begin your new role. It is common for first-time managers to be promoted out of the ranks they will now be managing.

Brad's approach in this book is to provide you with the relevant knowledge, skills and attitudes or worldview that will give you a chance to succeed in your new role as a manager or leader. When we worked at the Ken Blanchard Companies to create our first time manager program, we interviewed dozens of managers in the months after they made the transition from individual contributor to manager. The two strongest trends we heard in our interviews were how much of a shock it was transitioning to manager and how little practical knowledge was included in the transition.

Brad provides a comprehensive set of ideas, skills, perspectives and prospective attitudes for new leaders and managers to consider ensuring this critical transition is as effective and painless as possible.

Scott Blanchard
EVP and Principal of the Ken Blanchard Companies

HAVE YOU RECENTLY BEEN PROMOTED OR REASSIGNED TO A LEADERSHIP POSITION?

ARE YOU READY?

Many believe leaders are born and not made. Others believe it takes training, mentoring and practice to become an effective leader or manager today. Whether you are a believer in nature or nurture or a combination of the two, the time to get ready to lead is now.

Just what is leadership and why are its concepts sometimes so difficult to grasp? Why is it we know a good leader when we see one but all too often see so-called leaders who don't behave as we think they should? How can we hurry along the learning process to lead a team, division or a department?

I would like to offer you two options to attain the level of leadership needed to take up a new leadership position in 30 days.

1. Attend our live course; (see information at: https://quick-leadershipgroup.com.)

2. Read this book, based on a summary of essential leadership models, concepts, tools, and the experiences I've generated through 40+ years of leadership consulting, training, and practice.

Let me take you through a month-long learning adventure that will prepare you to assume the mantle of leadership! *Quick! I Need to Be a Leader in 30 Days!* asks you to keep an open mind, be willing to try new behaviors, and commit yourself to becoming the leader you always wanted to be—and the one your new followers deserve.

For the live course, each week brings a new Quick Leadership Group instructor to provide participants with live online instruction in various leadership models, tools and concepts. The clock is ticking, so instruction will be practical, to the point, and focused directly on immediate applications on the job.

Like the live course, this book takes a similar approach. Each chapter represents a week of training and describes the models, tools and concepts a new leader needs to "hit the ground running" in his or her new position. Each chapter offers readers a checklist and suggested on-the-job assignments to focus efforts on the application of leadership principles and practices.

In the course, a Strategic Leadership Advisor (SLA) conducts an end-of-the-week debriefing for each participant to discuss successes and challenges while carrying out leadership practices on the job. At the end of each chapter, this book also provides readers with a list of potential SLA discussion topics for their consideration, review and perhaps debriefings with a coach or mentor.

Successful participants of the "Quick! I Need to Be a Leader in 30 Days!" course can earn a Quick Leadership Group (QLG) Professional Leadership Certificate. Certificate criteria and course requirements are listed in Chapter Five: Leading into the Future.

There are many books available to readers on the subject of leadership. A list of the key leadership books that complement the subject matter and the approaches shared in this book is available in the reference section. This book also aids the experienced leader who needs a refresher and a reminder of some of the basics of leadership.

Please enjoy reading about acquiring the skills, knowledge and attitudes for becoming a new leader or manager. The decision to include or exclude leadership content is challenging and open to debate. Learning how to become a more effective leader is a life-long journey and, if you're lucky, a real adventure that can take you from leading a small team, to a government department, to a non-profit agency, to the leadership of a development project halfway around the world.

Let's get started!

"Leaders should be collaborative, modest, and generous."

—BILL BRADLEY
Former U.S. Senator & NBA Star

QUICK! I NEED TO BE A LEADER IN 30 DAYS!

Welcome! You are about to embark upon a 30-day journey to become an effective leader. How is that possible? Can leaders really be developed in only 30 days? Yes—if you are willing to make the effort!

The "Quick! I Need to Be a Leader in 30 Days!" course and this book are based on the following model of effective leadership.

THE QUICK LEADERSHIP MODEL

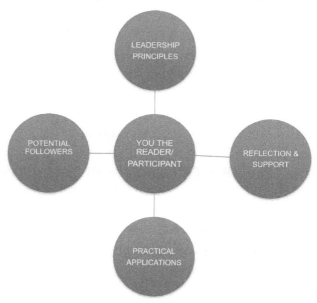

READER/PARTICIPANT: The focus of this book is on the reader/course participant, and at various points those terms will be used interchangeably. By equipping you with basic leadership skills, knowledge and attitudes, you will be enabled to begin your new position and take on new responsibilities with confidence and the ability to get the job done, all while providing inspiration, direction and support to followers.

LEADERSHIP PRINCIPLES: This includes the models, concepts, tools and tenets of leadership. Live, online instruction from Quick Leadership Group faculty members each week of the 4-week course enables participants to rapidly integrate the most critical principles of leadership. Readers will be introduced to these models through each book chapter.

POTENTIAL FOLLOWERS: This includes direct reports, coworkers, peers, colleagues, supervisors, executives, clients, stakeholders and anyone else who interface with new leaders and managers. Instruction focuses on developing trust and utilizing leadership tools such as temperament, conflict management, mass influence and Emotional Intelligence to develop more effective personal relationships.

PRACTICAL APPLICATIONS: Each week, on-the-job applications of the leadership principles that are discussed via online instruction or in book chapters are assigned as "homework." This book describes suggested application tasks and assignments that course participants are required to complete to become certified. Readers are urged to complete these assignments as integral parts of their self-directed leadership study.

REFLECTION & SUPPORT: While practical applications of leadership principles are of paramount importance to readers and participants for making instruction relevant and useful, applications of these principles requires personal reflection through journaling and weekly discussions to ensure a strong connection between theory and reality. Additionally, course participants need support for their efforts and the Quality Leadership Group's Strategic Leadership Advisor (SLA) provides it through weekly debriefings and assignment reviews. Readers are encouraged to identify a coach or mentor to provide a similar level of support, if possible.

GETTING READY

This book identifies the most effective leadership models, tools and concepts I've worked with through more than 40 years spent as a trainer, consultant, manager and author however, no one understands or applies these classic leadership approaches and implements them in the same way.

For example, I don't implement Situational Leadership exactly the way Ken Blanchard does. I do it my way, as influenced by Ken Blanchard. I don't apply conflict management principles exactly as Ralph Kilmann. I do it my way, as influenced by Ralph Kilmann. I don't implement *The Five Practices Of Exemplary Leadership* exactly as James Kouzes. I do it my way, as influenced by James Kouzes. And that's the way I recommend you take the information from this book.

In describing these practical leadership models and approaches, I've added my own viewpoints, practices and context for them. I like the metaphor of the leadership "toolbox." We each have a leadership toolbox and constantly add new tools, techniques and methods to it. When the situation warrants, we delve into our toolbox and pull out the model or tool we need and apply it our way.

I have found, when it comes to leadership, there is no "right" way to lead. We must all improvise and adapt to deal with the situation at hand and use whatever tools we have available to get us through the moment. So, it's in our best interest to load up our toolboxes with as many ideas, concepts, models, approaches and techniques we can find.

Developing and growing into an effective leader is a never-ending journey because it seems we never quite reach the finish line. We never attain leadership perfection. Just when we become proficient with the assortment of leadership tools in our toolbox, a new challenge develops and we must search for a new tool to address it.

For me, the challenge to match a leadership tool to a given situation represents the excitement and complexity of leadership. You and I may have the same tools at our disposal and virtually the same situation, but what works well for you may not work for me. Why is that? Is your application of the tool superior to mine? Is it my inability to apply the tool correctly in the situation? What really matters is that we recognize our task is to make the best tool selection from our toolbox and address the situation to our best ability.

This book provides the new leader or manager with guidance for understanding basic concepts while suggesting activities that build self-confidence, expand influencing networks and apply basic leadership tools on the job. Whether you use these tools the same way I do or not is immaterial. The struggle is to understand the basics, practice them on the job when you can and get support while you're doing it. Are you ready to take the leadership challenge?

As you start this book, take a look at the five most critical requirements needed to prepare for the daunting task of effective leadership described below. What you'll see is that the material I will present is not difficult to grasp, and actually quite logical and easily understood yet its application can be difficult and complex. Leadership is a time-consuming journey that can stoke the creative juices and screams at you to do more for your followers, coworkers, colleagues, executives and stakeholders.

#1 KEEP AN OPEN MIND

Throughout this book and the live course, readers and participants are exposed to a variety of leadership models, constructs, roles, opinions and on-the-job assignments that may not fit their idea of what an effective leader is supposed to do, be or look like. Take a deep breath and acknowledge that your leadership journey may take you to places you never expected to go.

Keeping an open mind will help you fill your "leadership toolbox" and decide, based on the situation, which leadership model, tool or concept you wish to use. It's anticipated you will end up modifying, adapting, tailoring and even developing tools of your own to fit your specific needs. Some concepts and tools may be entirely new to you while others will be modifications or adaptations of what you've learned through personal experiences or from other leadership trainings or readings.

#2 WILLINGLY TRY SOME NEW BEHAVIORS

Are you an introvert? As a member of a team or group, are you the last person to ask a question when everyone else is silent? Or are you an extrovert? As a member of a team or group, are you the first person to say something when everyone else is silent?

Expect your new leadership role to require new behaviors. For example, the introvert may be expected to offer opinions and ask questions when a team or group is quiet and fumbling; the extrovert may be expected to remain silent when a team is effectively working its way through a problem on its own. Initially some new leadership behaviors and techniques may be uncomfortable or even appear inappropriate, however over time and with more

25

understanding and practice, they become easier to perform and the leader becomes more effective.

#3 LEARN ABOUT YOURSELF

Learning how to lead is really all about self-knowledge: learning how you view the world; learning how and why you react to some people one way and to others another way; and, learning why some people just tick you off all the time! In Chapter 1: The Basic Elements® of Temperament serves as a guide for exploring what makes us tick and what we can do to treat followers the way they want to be treated—not as we want to treat them. An understanding that in any group or team there are followers with, potentially, four differing dominant temperaments enables the reader to tailor speeches, discussions, assignments and tasks that acknowledge the preferences and differences of staff and employees.

#4 PRACTICE, PRACTICE, PRACTICE

The leadership course itself involves live learning sessions with Quality Leadership Group (QLG) faculty members who have years of practical leadership experience as well as many years of training and team leadership. They'll introduce participants to a number of leadership models and approaches and describe various applications of effective—as well as ineffective—leadership practices. In the live course participants explore these leadership models in more depth by practicing them in real time through weekly assignments. They discuss what worked and what didn't with their Strategic Leadership Advisor (SLA), who'll serve as a mentor throughout the program.

Readers can review course content in this book and not only learn about basic leadership models and approaches but also apply them in on-the-job situations by following the weekly assignments and checklists provided at the end of each chapter. Without practice, there can really be no success.

An intensive one-month course builds on participant success. Practice sessions for readers and participants may range from discussing a course topic with a coworker or follower, to completing a checklist of activities, to leading a team meeting. A personal assessment of progress and leadership success is conducted weekly through conversations with the SLA or the reader's coach or mentor.

#5 STRIVE TO CERTIFY

The "Quick! I Need to Be a Leader in 30 Days!" certificate course requires the qualifying professional to demonstrate capability in these areas: Leadership Content Mastery, Commitment, Continuous Improvement, Integrity, Teamwork, Openness, Empowerment and Timeliness (see Chapter 5: Leading into the Future). No matter one's vision, mission, goals, objectives, strategies, budgets or action plans, it's the people in the organization who make everything happen and followers are a main focus of the Quick Leadership Model as are You, the Reader.

When a new leader assumes his/her role, it's easy to become bogged down with organizational bureaucracy, chains of command and personnel issues that consume time and energy. While being busy may make the new leader or manager feel they're doing great work and adding value to the organization, it pales in comparison to the need of leaders to rapidly establish positive relationships with employees.

The certification course that this book is based on covers a lot of ground in a short period of time. Included in this book is a day-by-day description of how and what the 30-day program covers (see Chapter 6: Quick Leadership 30-Day Guide).

In order to achieve the QLG Professional Leadership Certificate, course participants are expected to do their best through all the weekly activities and assignments and strive to complete their work in a timely and professional manner. The Strategic Leadership Advisor (SLA) evaluates participant competence and commitment to completing the course. Readers can utilize a coach or mentor to rate their own performance.

There are a number of additional requirements for the live course, including an Impact Paper and a 3-, 6- and 12-month action plan highlighting future leadership development and the application of effective leadership practices on the job (see Chapter 5: Leading into the Future).

Welcome to the start of your leadership journey. If you are willing to keep an open mind, try new behaviors, learn about yourself, practice what you've learned and strive to complete all the QLG Professional Leadership certification criteria, I am confident you will become an effective leader and go on to lead successful organizations.

Good luck!

Brad Dude, October, 2017

"Nothing will work unless you do."

—Maya Angelou
American Poet & Civil Rights Activist

CHAPTER ONE

WEEK 1:
LEADING
YOURSELF

A re you ready to become a leader in 30 days? Where do we start? We start with you of course: the reader—the individual.

Understanding how you see the world is a critical first step along the path to becoming an effective leader. How do you see your organization and the people who work within it? And how do you picture yourself fitting in as a new leader? It's entirely possible you've been promoted to this new position because of technical prowess demonstrated in the past. There's nothing wrong with that! It's a common road to the top of any organization.

In most companies, traditional "technical" knowledge describes expertise in whatever the business happens to be engaged (engineering, education, nursing, legal, law enforcement, welding.) However, the "technical" knowledge that leadership mastery requires means something different.

Researchers and authors James Kouzes and Barry Posner found traditional technical knowledge of leaders often fades away over time and unfortunately becomes the justification for micromanagers. How does this happen?

Over time technical capabilities decrease. Effective leadership is time-consuming. The incredible amount of effort spent on leadership and management tasks simply prevents leaders from remaining at the cutting edge of the technical skill sets they once possessed. Yet such leaders, equipped with ebbing skill sets, begin to search for something to do, and that often means looking over the shoulder of those followers doing the technical work in which they were once so skilled. Comments, suggestions and alternative technical approaches emanating from such micromanaging leaders drive followers and employees crazy and can ruin organizational morale.

Have you ever dealt with a micromanager? Often you either learn to avoid them or you end up submitting everything to them for their "blessing" or approval. A workforce that continually waits for micromanager approval of each and every task is usually demoralized and regularly missing deadlines. Micromanaging is not the way an effective leader operates.

Avoiding the pitfalls of micromanagement requires an understanding and an exploration of personal skills, abilities, and attitudes toward one's new leadership position. So, how is it decided what new leaders should work on in order to avoid the pitfalls of micromanagement?

PERSONAL SKILL CHALLENGES

Read through these two lists of activities and decide which ones: 1) You are doing OK with; 2) You should do more of; 3) You should do less of; and, 4) You need to start doing. You also can add your own skills or behaviors to the list. When you finish, identify 3-5 skills you would like to focus on over the next month. Your Strategic Leadership Advisor, coach or mentor should review your progress at the end of each course week.

	OK	DO MORE	DO LESS	START DOING
COMMUNICATION SKILLS				
1. SEEKING, GIVING, & RECEIVING FEEDBACK				
2. STAYING ON POINT				
3. CONTROLLING EXTROVERTS IN MEETINGS				
4. DRAWING OUT INTROVERTS IN MEETINGS				
5. ACTIVE LISTENING				
6. COMFORT WITH PUBLIC SPEAKING				
7. RECAPPING CONVERSATIONS TO ENSURE CLARITY AND ACCURACY				
8. ONE-ON-ONE CONVERSATIONS				
9.				
MORALE-BUILDING SKILLS				
10. DEMONSTRATING PERSONAL INTEREST IN OTHERS				
11. ENSURING FULL PARTICIPATION				
12. REACHING CONSENSUS OR AGREEMENT				
13. REDUCING GROUP STRESS & TENSION				
14. SUPPORTING MINORITY VIEWPOINTS IN GROUP DISCUSSIONS				
15. DEMONSTRATING APPRECIATION OR PRAISE				
16.				
17.				
EMOTIONAL EXPRESSIVENESS				
18. EXPRESSING PERSONAL OPINIONS				
19. SHOWING EMPATHY				
20. UTILIZING EMOTIONAL INTELLIGENCE				

	OK	DO MORE	DO LESS	START DOING
21. Acknowledging people for superior work efforts				
22. Understanding personal temperament				
23. Handling conflict				
24.				
25.				
Other				

PERSONAL DEVELOPMENT CHALLENGES

	OK	DO MORE	DO LESS	START DOING
Social Relationships				
1. Competing with others				
2. Dominating conversations when needed				
3. Establishing trust with others				
4. Supporting staff and employees				
5. Protecting employees from bureaucracy				
6. Standing up for your own position				
7. Initiating private conversations				
8.				
9.				

OBSERVATIONS SKILLS				
10. DIAGNOSING TEAM DEVELOPMENT STAGES				
11. NOTICING CHANGES IN LEADERSHIP DURING MEETINGS				
12. NOTICING GROUP DYNAMICS IN MEETINGS				
13. DIAGNOSING PROCESS FLAWS				
14. NOTICING GROUP LEVELS OF ENERGY				
15. OBSERVING WHO IS PARTICIPATING AND WHO IS NOT				
16. NOTING NONVERBAL REACTIONS (POSITIVE AND NEGATIVE)				
17.				
18.				
GENERAL				
19. ASKING FOR HELP				
20. BALANCING WORK/LIFE REQUIREMENTS				
21. REDUCING PERSONAL STRESS				
22. ACCEPTING PERSONAL CRITICISM				
23. UNDERSTANDING YOUR JOB				
24. DEALING WITH BUREAUCRACY AND DELAYS				
25.				
26.				
OTHER				

LEADERSHIP VS. MANAGEMENT

Too many organizations view the role of leader and manager as virtually the same. They are not. Practically, however, there are few organizations that have positions titled, "Leader." Managers or executives are typically expected to serve as leaders as well as being responsible for the more classic managerial duties of planning, budgeting, organizing, staffing, controlling and problem solving. So, when do they have time to be leaders?

Leadership tasks, too often, do not get done at all. Activities such as setting direction, aligning people and providing a work environment that motivates others to do exceptional work, are often left to annual strategic planning meetings and then not followed through with or done without input from anyone other than a few individuals ensconced in an executive suite or the president's office—behind closed doors. This means managers end up trying to control things in the short-term with little time to think about a vision for the organization or the tasks that need to be done immediately to prepare their team, division, department or company for an ever-changing future.

It's recognized today managers wear two hats. They must wear a manager's hat, but they also must carve out time and effort to don a leader's hat as well. So, what are the differences between leadership and management? Dr. James Colvard, a former director of the Naval Surface Warfare Center/Dahlgren Division (NSWCDD) and John P. Kotter, a noted author and Harvard professor of leadership, identify the classic differences this way:

LEADERSHIP (COPING WITH RAPID CHANGE)	MANAGEMENT (COPING WITH COMPLEXITY)
Setting Direction	Planning & Budgeting
Aligning People	Organizing & Staffing
Providing an Environment that Motivates Others	Controlling & Problem-Solving

Colvard and Kotter agree leadership complements management and, although the basic functions of each go hand-in-hand (and you can't have good leadership and poor management, nor poor leadership and good management, and succeed), each role handles these tasks in different ways.

Leaders and managers all strive to articulate what goals, tasks and activities need to be completed; struggle to recruit, train and support a cadre of personnel to carry out those goals, tasks and activities; and, finally, strain to support, supervise, measure and evaluate these personnel and their progress. Leaders, however, may focus on setting a vision for the future and identifying the type of strategies and changes needed to guide their organizations toward that vision. Leaders also concern themselves with identifying the skills, knowledge and temperament needed in personnel to enhance and strengthen the organization's capabilities in the future, and leaders inspire the workforce by providing the necessary work environment that can self-motivate followers.

Colvard has expanded his thinking on the differences between the roles of leaders and managers in the following chart:

LEADERS	MANAGERS
Do the right things	Do things right
Challenge existing systems and search for methods of continuous improvement	Minimize risk and keep systems operating efficiently
Produce useful change	Deal with resistance to change
Formulate and ask probing questions	Find answers and solutions
Live in large webs of relationships	Deal with organizational relations and a changing workforce
See where there is no light; hear when there is no sound	See and hear what is going on
Design and lead change efforts	Carry out change
Motivate and inspire employees	Push employees in the right direction

Leaders	Managers
Long-term oriented	Short-term oriented
Develop vision and strategies	Obtain clear performance improvements and achieve objectives

Often, leaders will not know for years if their decisions were correct or if they actually pay off. When Colvard was approached by his former organization for permission to name a leadership award after him, he told them, "Check back in 10 years to see if you still want to do that." They did, and there's now a leadership award named after him at NSWCDD.

Again, an organization requires effective and efficient leaders and managers. The responsibilities and duties of each often reside in such titles as *manager, director* or *branch chief*. It's common for people to view leaders as managers and managers as leaders. The higher one goes in company hierarchies, the more one is expected to demonstrate leadership—no matter their actual title.

Are you a manager with newly acquired leadership responsibilities? Great! Experienced managers already know their technical skills are dwindling; and, they're dependent on followers to produce real work. The most critical part of their job is to identify and eliminate various inhibitors preventing employees from doing their jobs effectively and efficiently. Plus, understanding how to obtain and use power and influence is critical to the success of any leader or manager.

Kotter also writes highly successful managers recognize their dependency on others. In a competitive environment, managers vie with their counterparts in other divisions and departments for limited resources and often have no direct control over the people who make decisions about those resources. That's where the use of power comes into play.

TYPES OF POWER

There are three types of power, according to Colvard, in the context of leadership and management. They are: Power of Position, Power of Competence and the Power of Positive Reputation.

Power of Position: Haven't you always wanted to be the boss and sit at the summit of the organizational pyramid? To be at the top of the food chain—the leader of the pack? Yet the Power of Position is considered by author John Maxwell to be the lowest form of power. Why? Although it's needed to avoid chaos and create order it's a form of power based on the threat of negative consequences for those who disobey it.

What are examples of the Power of Position in society today? Police officers, judges, the Internal Revenue Service, and the military all possess this power. You can recognize them by their badges, uniforms, robes, or stripes. While they play critical and vital roles in society by providing structure, upholding laws and rules, and maintaining order, their authority is based on *controlling* rather than *motivating.* This power is most effective at controlling observable actions and, to be effective, requires enforcement provisions. For example, if you're observed speeding and ticketed, what happens if you don't pay? You are fined and your license may be revoked. If speeding laws were not enforced, you might always be disobeying them. Colvard points out that a corollary of this power is that it is not meant for personal use. The holders of Position Power who abuse it or use it for personal gain may be fined or imprisoned—or both!

What about leaders and managers with Position Power? They can be recognized by their perks: corner or larger offices, personal assistants and/or secretaries, company cars, stock options, private dining rooms. For example a Chief Executive Officer (CEO) relies almost totally on others to produce work since it would be impossible for him/her to directly observe the entire workforce each day. So Position Power is delegated down to directors, managers, branch chiefs, and team leaders on behalf of the CEO. The workforce understands that disobedience to certain orders may result in a demotion, removal from a plum assignment, reassignment, being passed up for a promotion or even fired. Controlling rather than motivating the workforce is not very effective when dealing with tasks that depend on mental rather than physical activity because it is not necessarily observable.

Members of management who abuse their power (e.g., unfairly ordering employees to do something simply because they're "the boss," absconding with company funds, or otherwise use their power for personal gain) may also be dismissed, fined or imprisoned. Abusers of Position Power may also experience resistance to their authority in the forms of passive-aggressive employee behavior, organizational sabotage, or even mass resignations.

According to Colvard, the most important characteristic of the Power of Position is that it remains within the organization and does not travel with the individual. When an admiral retires from the Navy, his power to approve budgets and send ships to distant ports also retires. When a CEO moves on to another job or retires, the power she personally held within her organization to hire or fire and make decisions immediately vanishes and transfers to the next CEO.

Power of Competence: Unlike the Power of Position, this power may grow and remain with the individual throughout his/her career regardless of a new position or organization. This power is gained and enhanced in four major ways—and you only have total control over one of them.

1. Inherent Capability (inborn capabilities and ability to generate energy)

2. Personal Attitude (individual has total control)
3. Formal (and Informal) Education
4. Real-World Experience

Let's think about how this power applies to you as a new leader. You are born with some inherent capability and an inherent ability to generate energy and enthusiasm. Inborn temperament also is a factor and an influence on your behavior and worldview. (Thank your parents for all that and remember you did nothing to earn this capability!)

Colvard reminds us that some people are born with inherent capability and choose to do nothing with it. Their personal attitudes are so poor they do not grow or enhance their inherent capability (Colvard assesses their Power of Competence to be zero).

As a new leader striving to become effective in 30 days, your personal attitude, the one thing you have total control over, is obviously positive and you are now demonstrating your willingness to learn more about leadership by reading this book, thereby enhancing your inherent capability.

Your Power of Competence is also enhanced through Formal and Informal Education and Real-World Experiences, although you did not have total control over any of them. For example, if your grades weren't great or your funds were limited, perhaps you didn't get into the school you most wanted. If your supervisor needed you to stay behind at the office while others got to attend an important technical conference, you may have missed out on a great learning experience. Although you may have had some influence, you didn't have total control over your education and work experience. While your inherent capabilities, energy and personal attitude were ready and willing, the opportunities may not have presented themselves quite the way you wanted.

Leaders today often move on to 3-5 positions throughout their careers and, as stated earlier, they always take with them their Power of Competence. Each training course, seminar, and webinar attended—every article, blog and book read—adds to one's Power of Competence. Many leaders have said it's not so much the education and the experiences (which they typically enjoy) but rather, it's maintaining their personal attitude over time that's most challenging.

New leaders should remember, as they begin their new jobs (Power of Position), to keep their eyes open for opportunities to develop their followers. They too are on journeys to enhance their Power of Competence and need to have real-world experiential opportunities to build upon their inherent capabilities. There are too many stories of employees with tremendous inherent capability and fantastic personal attitudes who never get the opportunity to excel. Ensure that you are not one of those "leaders" who deny followers opportunities to gain experience just because you're exercising the Power of Position!

Power of Positive Reputation: Everyone wants to have a great reputation, right? It's the ultimate form of individual power and one's reputation, whether positive or negative, never leaves one's side. Most importantly, it travels wherever one works. It becomes a critical means for others to identify and perceive the status of a leader. The Power of Positive Reputation is earned by doing the job effectively and efficiently, by developing others, by continually honing their leadership expertise and by walking the talk—doing what one says they'll do—consistently over time. It's gaining the trust of others.

A great reputation takes many years to develop and makes it easy for the leaders and managers who possess it to persuade and influence followers, colleagues, supervisors, clients, suppliers, stakeholders and executives to act on their behalf, especially to adopt change. No titles are needed. No formal Position Power or direct control is necessary. Author John Maxwell calls this the highest level of leadership and writes that people will follow because of who you are and what you represent.

> *"It takes twenty years to build a reputation and five minutes to ruin it. If you think about that, you'll do things differently."*
>
> —Warren Buffett
> *American Business Magnate & Investor*

Recall that leaders and managers recognize their dependency on others. Armed with the Power of Positive Reputation, it's easily understandable how the trust and respect they receive from others within and without the organization support their work efforts. They've proven themselves over and over again to be trustworthy, honest and willing to support others and their institutions. Why wouldn't they receive any and all the help they need or desire, within the capabilities of those they're asking for assistance? Achieving this level of power should be a career goal of every new leader and manager.

The Power of Positive Reputation is not just an individual power. It's also highly impactful on organizational power also known as "corporate culture." It's the unwritten "way things are done around here."

Do you know of a company that's perceived by customers, employees, and the public for living its culture? Southwest Airlines, for example, is great at communicating its vision to employees who have the green light to do whatever is reasonably necessary to meet customer demands. Facebook has a competitive culture and utilizes open workspaces to give employees an equal chance to succeed. Twitter hosts a team-oriented working environment to motivate employees who love their work and the organization's many perks.

A review of all three of these types of power leads one to understand that the path to obtaining and using power most effectively is not through a promotion to a leadership position but rather by having earned it through the process of living an honorable life, adding skills and experiences, and helping others.

> *"In the past, a leader was a boss. Today's leader must be a partner with their people . . . they no longer can lead solely based on positional power."*
>
> —KEN BLANCHARD
> *Coauthor of "Leadership & the One Minute Manager"*

FOUR FATAL FEARS

The concept of "Leading Yourself" focuses on some of the fears you may possess that are inhibiting you from taking action, making decisions or giving and receiving feedback. A leader who's reluctant to take a stand on an issue or act when actions are needed will hinder their organization and becomes a liability.

> *"Whatever you fear most has no power—it is your fear that has the power."*
>
> —OPRAH WINFREY
> *American Businesswoman & Talk Show Host*

The late psychologist Maxie Maultsby, Jr. named four deeply felt fears that can be fatal for a leader who cannot overcome them.

These fears can prevent the gaining of trust and can inhibit the ability to interact with others. Organizations also can be immobilized when their leaders suffer from these Four Fatal Fears:

Fear of Failure

Fear of Being Wrong

Fear of Rejection

Fear of Being Emotionally Uncomfortable

Fear of Failure: If leaders (or their followers) suffer from this fear, it means they have a strong need to succeed. In order to meet this need, they may be reluctant to take on new or challenging assignments; appear over eager to take on easy tasks; be risk-averse; and, interpret everything as all-or-nothing propositions.

> **Strategy:** Change the mindset from anticipating failure to doing the best you can. Rather than focusing on failure, believe there are only learning experiences that will add to inherent capabilities.

Fear of Being Wrong: If leaders (or their followers) suffer from this fear, it means they have a strong need to be right. To meet this need, they may be reluctant to participate in meetings; dominate and control discussions; discount the creative ideas of others; and, remain silent for long periods of time.

> **Strategy:** Realize you don't know everything and accept it. Release expectations of perfection. Identify knowledge resources in technical areas where you are weaker and rely on them for assistance.

Fear of Rejection: If leaders (or their followers) suffer from this fear, it means they have a strong need to be accepted. In order to meet this need, they may be unwilling to question the views of others; avoid personal confrontations at all costs; become a "people pleaser;" give only positive performance evaluations or avoid them entirely; become antisocial; rely on consensus decision making; and, crave to be liked more than respected.

> **Strategy:** Build up self-confidence (see Chapter Four: Week 3: Optional Practicum). Disclose your opinions, thoughts and ideas, especially in areas of strength. Practice the soliciting, giving and receiving of feedback.

Fear of Being Emotionally Uncomfortable: If leaders (or their followers) suffer from this fear, it means they have a strong need to be comfortable. To meet this need, they may be avoiding emotions in the workplace; are unable to respond to the emotional needs of followers; feel lonely and isolated while stress levels rise; are reluctant to make decisions due to potential emotional reactions; and, miss opportunities to connect at a more in-depth level with coworkers.

> **Strategy:** Take small steps by focusing on an easy goal or task just outside the comfort zone. Build on successes and put yourself into situations requiring the discussion of workplace emotions—either your own or the emotions of others.

Another fear that has been discovered in the age of social media, cell phones, and laptops is the FEAR OF MISSING OUT: FOMO. New leaders and managers particularly suffer from this fear since they often feel a strong need to always know what's happening in their teams, branches, divisions and departments as they begin their leadership careers.

In recent years, many leadership workshop participants bring up the need to always be in touch with their work, no matter the time, date, place, evenings, weekends, and holidays—even during their vacations.

Although most organizations officially do not require communication access and accessibility to all its leaders on a 24/7 basis, many of our leadership workshop participants believe they'll end up *behind the promotion curve* if they don't maintain this all-encompassing level of communication and personal availability. Such discussions frequently evolve into work/life balance debates and the toll such perceived after-hours contact demands have on family life.

Each leader must evaluate how to deal best with FOMO as they progress in their career. A strategy for dealing with this fear may be as simple as discussing communication and availability requirements with supervisors and executives. However, while *official* requirements do not always exist, the career-minded leader (and other key employees) may tackle FOMO in other ways (e.g., arranging for colleagues to send text notices over holidays, identifying alternate points of contact to provide updates at prescribed dates and times, and scheduling online meetings during off hours to stay informed of office issues).

Leaders need to overcome all their fears in order to effectively provide the vision, support and guidance their organizations and followers need. It is recognized that fears are a long time in the making and take a long time to exorcise. Effective leaders acknowledge how these fears may act as inhibitors to fulfilling their leadership goals. Turning fears and their negative mindsets into strategies of positive potential and innovation is truly a huge leadership undertaking.

> *"Don't permit fear of failure to prevent effort. We are all imperfect and will fail on occasions, but fear of failure is the greatest failure of all."*
>
> —JOHN WOODEN
> *Hall of Fame Basketball Coach, UCLA*

THE BASIC ELEMENTS® OF TEMPERAMENT

One tool that examines inner motivations and provides an explanation for how (and why) you view your workplace, job, boss, followers and colleagues the way you do is called the Basic Elements of Temperament. This tool is used throughout the live course and this book to assist readers in self-assessment and for understanding personal reactions to the behaviors observed in a team or organization.

Temperament is that inborn part of the personality that influences the way one views the world and how one reacts to observable behaviors. Developed by Jim Harden and myself in our first book, *"What Makes You Tick and What Ticks You Off: How the Basic Elements of Temperament Will Lead You to a Happier Life,"* this model stresses the understanding of four temperament elements which we call Earth, Air, Fire and Water.

Let's look at each of the four temperaments, remembering that everyone possesses all four of them, ranked in a hierarchical order at birth. Like a stack of plates in a restaurant, the top plate, or dominant temperament, may be any of the four. The second, called the secondary temperament, comes next, followed by the third, or tertiary temperament. The last plate in the hierarchical stack is called the shadow temperament. Let's review each of the four basic elements and see how their characteristics can help new leaders and managers learn more about how they are predisposed to lead.

Earth Temperament: Individuals with dominant Earth temperaments want to see all the available facts and understand the realities of any situation. They want to organize these facts to design specific plans for making the right decisions to help their followers, teams, branches, divisions, departments and/or organizations. Earths take great pride in their institutions and will protect them at all costs. That means protecting organizational resources, personnel, customers and even reputations. Dominant Earths are realistic, practical and decisive. They follow rules and regulations and are often the ones who make them. They're detail-oriented and dependable. Their word is their bond.

However, Earths are skeptical of others who want to change processes, schemes and strategies without a justifiable reason. They'll not break rules for one person, because they'd have to break them for everyone else, too. Earths are impatient and typically establish strict deadlines for deliverables and progress reports.

They're unafraid of making a quick decision based on the information at hand. Followers, and others, must earn their trust by proving they're capable of following directions and getting work done on time, on budget, and all the while communicating progress in a timely manner.

Air Temperament: Dominant Air temperaments view their organizations as having great potential and endless possibilities for success. They like to spend time calmly examining these possibilities analytically and impersonally and prefer to work alone or with just a few qualified colleagues. Airs are competent and expect their followers be, too. They have great vision and are able to articulate what teams, branches, divisions, departments and even their organizations will look like in 10 or 20 years. Airs can identify the type of changes that are needed to make their vision a reality. When someone tells an Air, "It can't be done," that's when dominant Airs really enjoy proving they can complete the task. They set high standards for themselves and others. Airs are great designers of projects, task forces, and pilot programs.

However, Airs do not show much sensitivity and appreciation for the personal efforts of followers and other employees. They're not detail-oriented. They often fail to follow through as they promised because of boredom with needlessly bureaucratic processes. It's often difficult for followers to maintain the same level of focus and attention on complex issues that fascinate Airs so much. Airs are frequently perceived

as arrogant and elitists. When they don't view followers or colleagues as intellectually competent, they're
impatient and dismissive of them.

Fire Temperament: Dominant Fire temperaments
also want to see all the facts and realities of any situation, much like dominant Earth temperaments. Unlike
Earths, however, who want to utilize these facts for
planning and organizing purposes, the Fire temperament wants to collect even more facts and manipu-
late them for practical applications, resulting in solving problems in a fast, effective, timely and enjoyable
manner. Fires are great at troubleshooting and handling crisis situations. They're resourceful and know
how to get things done while avoiding bureaucratic
red tape and procedural norms. Fires are practical,
flexible and enjoy taking risks.

However, Fires are unpredictable. The way they handled a situation yesterday will be different from how
they handle it tomorrow. They're easily bored if there
are no crises to solve. They may even invent a crisis
to tackle. Fires dislike meetings and writing reports.
They're impulsive and leap before they look. Fires
would rather not wait until all options and theories
about a situation are discussed before taking action.

Water Temperament: Dominant Water temperaments see great potential and possibilities in their
followers and in their organizations, much like dominant Air temperaments. Unlike Airs, however, who
want to impersonally analyze the future of their organizations, Waters want to judge the value of these

possibilities against their impact on followers and other employees. They draw out the best in people. Waters will sacrifice evening hours and weekends to help a follower with a project. They're great at expressing sympathy and appreciation. They can easily influence others to work effectively together in harmony. Waters enjoy learning new skills and learning more about themselves and others.

However, Waters are almost too generous in giving up their time and effort for their organizations and followers. They often make decisions based on personal likes and dislikes. They're easily hurt by personal criticism. They take negative performance evaluations much too personally and often focus too much on the welfare of other people rather than the goals of their operating unit. Waters have a difficult time saying no to anyone.

Secondary and Tertiary Temperaments

While the effect of the tertiary temperament, the third temperament in the hierarchical stack of four basic elements, is typically neutral, the secondary temperament, the second plate in the stack, has an impact and strong influence in supporting the dominant temperament.

The secondary temperament is often confused with the dominant temperament. This is due to its typically satisfactory impact on the personality with the dominant temperament. Many readers new to temperament believe they possess two dominant temperaments. Research has shown, however, this is not the case. The secondary temperament, like the dominant, tertiary and shadow, is there because of neurotransmitter and hormone levels in the brain at birth. These include:

EARTH → SEROTONIN
AIR → TESTOSTERONE
FIRE → DOPAMINE
WATER → ESTROGEN

These inborn brain chemicals are enhanced and further developed by education and life experiences. In fact, all four temperaments are products of inherent brain chemistry enhanced by education and personal experiences. The overall goal of the study of the Basic Elements of Temperament is to further develop all four temperaments to use them as tools for becoming a more effective leader.

A developed secondary temperament can prevent new leaders from rushing headlong into potentially sticky situations their dominant temperaments tell them will be okay. Preventing leaders from jumping into the deep end of a situation requiring additional thought and consideration can be a real lifesaver and a helpful role of the secondary temperament.

Let's take a look at some examples of how the secondary temperament supports and influences the dominant temperament. Sometimes, it will compel the new leader to slow down before making an important decision. Sometimes, it will broaden their consideration of a bigger picture and situational context. And other times, it will tell leaders they do not have to take themselves so seriously.

In reviewing the following table, reflect upon personal education and experiences to identify a moment when your dominant temperament compelled a certain decision or line of thinking, but your secondary temperament influenced and compelled further consideration of the potential impact in which that decision might have resulted.

DOMINANT TEMPERAMENT	SECONDARY TEMPERAMENT	INFLUENCE OF SECONDARY ON DOMINANT TEMPERAMENT
EARTH	AIR	*Air secondary temperaments support examination of relevant information and influence competency in analysis.*
EARTH	FIRE	*Fire secondary temperaments influence the ability to more easily see humor in facts and realities of situations, and results in more personable leadership.*
EARTH	WATER	*Water secondary temperaments are reminders of the impact that organizing and planning have on followers.*
AIR	EARTH	*Earth secondary temperaments enhance awareness of the importance of meeting deadlines and achieving objectives.*
AIR	FIRE	*Fire secondary temperaments influence becoming more short-term focused and practical in decision-making.*
AIR	WATER	*Water secondary temperaments increase awareness of enhanced employee competence and skill and increase awareness of learning opportunities.*
FIRE	EARTH	*Earth secondary temperaments increase awareness of more traditional approaches before trying something "out of the box."*
FIRE	AIR	*Air secondary temperaments suggest a more reason-based approach to rapidly getting things done.*

DOMINANT TEMPERAMENT	SECONDARY TEMPERAMENT	INFLUENCE OF SECONDARY ON DOMINANT TEMPERAMENT
FIRE	WATER	*Water secondary temperaments enhance understanding and consideration for the feelings of others.*
WATER	EARTH	*Earth secondary temperaments influence consideration of the greater organizational good on decisions that may negatively impact employees.*
WATER	AIR	*Air secondary temperaments serve as reminders that a logical approach can aid in making emotional decisions.*
WATER	FIRE	*Fire secondary temperaments influence more openness to taking risks and using non-traditional methods.*

Shadow Temperament

An aspect of the Basic Elements of Temperament is working with the shadow temperament, that is, one's fourth temperament in the hierarchical stack. The fascination with the shadow has been around a long time.

Back in 1886 when *"Strange Case of Dr. Jekyll and Mr. Hyde"* by Robert Louis Stevenson was published readers understood the internal and external struggle between good and evil. This bolstered what many religions preached as well: *man is born sinful and must struggle and fight to find eternal happiness by choosing to be good and righteous.* Carl Jung, a noted Swiss psychiatrist and psychoanalyst, building on the work of Sigmund Freud, studied the shadow temperament and found that it contained positive as well as negative emotions dwelling within the unconscious mind.

Today, the Basic Elements of Temperament asks new leaders to explore their own shadow temperaments in a new way. While one's dominant temperament is the *most preferred* manner of be-having and viewing the world, one's shadow temperament is the *least preferred* manner of behaving and viewing the world—and often shows up at embarrassing times, such as at work when the behaviors of others are viewed from the shadow temperament's perspective and judged to be negative, harmful, wrong or stupid, simply because of the shadow's built-in bias against employing such behaviors.

As a leader, knowing how to identify the shadow temperament in others can be an effective method for aiding self-control and for avoiding needless confrontations and arguments. Remember, the behaviors one observes usually represent the dominant temper-ament of the person performing them. Some behaviors, however, represent the leader's shadow temperament—their least preferred behaviors and the ones she may view as inappropriate and wrong.

Let's review some examples of different *attitudes* held about each of the four temperaments to see if you can match any of them with your own. First will come a list of 20 perceived characteristics that exhibit what the shadow temperament might say or believe about each of the Basic Elements. Next are quotes from actual temperament-training participants describing their shadows. If your views match these attitudes, you have probably found your shadow temperament. Ready?

Earths are: parental, manipulative, judgmental, in-flexible, controlling, conservative, meticulous, un-imaginative, humorless, patronizing, strict, inflex-ible, hypercritical, precautionary, "In a rut," rigid, righteous, preventive, obstinate, and conventional.

"Earths are such control freaks and always insist that there is only one correct way to do something. I always

feel they have something more important to do when I'm with them and they believe my ideas are unprofessional or even juvenile. They always need to know what we're going to do before it even happens. They just treat me like I'm in kindergarten and haven't grown up yet."

Airs are: cold, unemotional, calculating, condescending, elitist, haughty, ruthless, unrealistic, devious, stubborn, arrogant, artificial, vain, conceited, sly, skeptical, scheming, heartless, callous, and cruel.

"Airs take too much time analyzing and take forever to make a decision. My work never meets their standards but they always forget to tell me a few critical things they need when they assign a job and can't follow through on the detailed things that I need. I wish just once they'd show some sensitivity or appreciation for what I do. When they discuss a matter, they go on and on and on."

Fires are: unreliable, reckless, untrustworthy, boorish, thrill-seekers, immature, unprofessional, cowboys, rash, gamblers, defiant, juvenile, buffoons, cynical, disobedient, obstinate, irregular, cutting and disorderly, and they march to the beat of their own drummer.

"Fires always seem to contradict previous decisions that they've made. They also don't focus on all of the details of a matter and can't seem to articulate the next steps and follow-up plans of a task they want you to do. They bore easily, and when I'm having difficulty, they

55

become impatient and start finishing my sentences.
I wish I could just predict how they will react to things.
They're so impulsive."

Waters are: emotional, nosy, meddlesome, chatty, time wasters, clinging, overly sensitive, prying, gossips, crusaders, snoops, opinionated, impractical, fragile, sentimental, idealistic, impulsive, eavesdroppers, interfering, and weak.

"It always seems that Waters are gossiping or at least poking into my feelings and my personal business. They're constantly fretting about whether or not their decisions will upset someone or make them mad. If you say something critical about their work, they take it as a personal attack. I wish they'd worry as much about the company's future as they do about the people. They just don't hold their people accountable or demand them to be disciplined in what they do."

Views from one's shadow temperament get leaders in the most trouble. When follower behaviors are judged from the shadow's perspective to be negative or harmful simply because of built-in preferences against employing such behaviors, leaders open themselves to accusations of playing favorites, discrimination, and bias.

Communicating with Different Temperaments

Hopefully the reader's identification of dominant, secondary, tertiary, and shadow temperaments is now complete. You can also get a good idea of the dominant temperaments of your co-workers, colleagues and supervisors by observing their behaviors on-the-job. Armed with this information, what is the best way to communicate with followers and other employees based on their temperaments? How can the Basic Elements of Temperament be used as a leadership tool without using it to *label* or *profile* people in the workforce?

In large temperament workshops, participants are divided into groups representing each of the four dominant temperaments. Each group discusses the various strengths and perceived myths that possessing their particular temperament bring to their work and their understanding of coworkers. Their conversations are low-key, professional and typically result in agreement about the value each temperament adds to the organization.

Later in the day, training participants visit a group representing their shadow temperament and discuss what they appreciated, if anything, about that temperament and the stumbling blocks they experience when dealing with people from that dominant temperament. Conversations in this grouping are different from the earlier session. In shadow groups with participants from that temperament serving as coaches, the conversations become much more lively and animated. Volume levels rise, as does laughter, high-pitched voices of arguers, and the low-pitched tones of serious questioners.

The shadow temperament discussion is often cited as the most helpful session experienced by workshop participants. A major lesson learned is that holding conversations with people from one's shadow temperament is a great way to understand what makes them tick. It also aids in developing one's own shadow temperament—often the temperament that is avoided or unacknowledged by leaders and followers alike. Freud and Jung believed the shadow temperament resided within one's unconscious. For many participants, it's the first time they've ever acknowledged the existence of their shadow and realized how it can negatively influence their relationships with others.

The shadow temperament also hides a positive aspect of interests, skills, and other talents that one has forgotten, cast aside as too difficult, or decided were out of reach. While a grown adult can no longer play second base for the Dodgers, he may be able to get in better shape, eat healthier, and coach a Little League team. Perhaps a grown adult can no longer become a millionaire. However, she may be able to balance a checkbook, purchase stocks, or make a budget. Developing the shadow temperament involves more than just understanding the sources of negative feelings, reactions, and negative attitudes. It also involves revisiting lost talents.

Let's take a look at what might be expected in communicating with each dominant temperament, all the while remembering that one of the temperaments represents your shadow.

DOMINANT TEMPERAMENT	COMMUNICATION IS:	THEY TALK ABOUT:	THEY WILL RESPOND BY:
EARTH	Built on facts Clear & precise Direct Succinct & to the point Bottom-line focused	Past accomplishments Personal responsibility Efficiency Realism in dealing with problems	Owning the conversation Developing plans & systems Acting quickly to solve a problem Keeping the status quo
AIR	Logical & concise Intellectual in use of vocabulary & explaining a vision Unaware of nonverbal cues Clever & precise Impersonal	Big picture Problem-solving Future directions Illogical policies & regulations Expectations for employees & management	Debating points of view Analyzing your position or idea Questioning your logic Asking to postpone decisions

DOMINANT TEMPERAMENT	COMMUNICATION IS:	THEY TALK ABOUT:	THEY WILL RESPOND BY:
FIRE	Operational & practical Humorous Wide-ranging Creative Innovative Problem-focused Scattered	Experiences Adventures New approaches/ strategies Methods for cutting bureaucratic corners Current projects that interest them	Brainstorming ideas Designing new methods Thinking "out of the box" Being excited about a new plan, project, or program
WATER	Honest Expressive Broad-based Aware of nonverbal cues Metaphorical Showing personal appreciation	Increasing harmony Personal issues Friends, family & coworkers Self-Improvement. Learning opportunities for others Helping the organization	Actively listening Being supportive of new ideas Volunteering to help Negotiating conflicts

Organizational Temperament

Can an organization have a dominant temperament? Although there are no inborn organizational preferences (unless they're in the eyes of their founders) companies also take on the characteristics of the four Basic Elements—mostly a single or dominant temperament. Institutional temperament often can be deciphered by analyzing slogans, logos, value declarations and mission statements. Look through the following examples to identify the organization's "dominant" temperament:

The Boy Scouts of America

"The mission of The Boy Scouts of America is to prepare young people to make ethical and moral choices over their lifetimes by instilling in them the values of the Scout Oath and Scout Law."

The Boy Scouts is an Earth organization. Why? Examine some of the words used in its mission statement: "prepare young people" (family-oriented); "make ethical and moral choices" (noble and conservative); and instill "values of the Scout Oath and Scout Law" (rules and regulations).

Google

"The mission of Google is to organize the world's information and make it universally accessible and useful."

Google is an Air organization. Look again at the mission statement: "world's information" (big picture and data-driven); "make it universally accessible and useful" (meanings, possibilities, and competence).

IDEO (Global Design Company)

"IDEO has developed seven human-centered values that characterize its corporate culture including: Be Optimistic; Collaborate; Embrace Ambiguity; Learn from Failure; Make Others Successful; Take Ownership; and Talk Less, Do More."

Although one could argue IDEO's values also could describe a Water organization, it's actually a Fire. IDEO boasts open workspaces, a flexible leadership hierarchy, revolving project leadership, lots of humor, and creative and innovative projects where "out of the box" thinking is not only encouraged but also expected of its workforce.

The Walt Disney Company

"The mission of the Walt Disney Company is to be one of the world's leading producers and providers of entertainment and information."

WEEK 1: LEADING YOURSELF

This one is a bit harder to decipher from its mission statement alone because it's such a large company with so many interests in the family entertainment business. However, knowing that it's involved in everything from sports (ESPN) to family movies (*Beauty and the Beast*) to theme parks (Disneyland and Disney World), and many other spinoffs, such as video games, cable TV, radio, tends to make it a Water organization—a people-first organization.

At the end of the first week of live instruction, participants will meet with their Strategic Leadership Advisor (SLA) by phone or online. The SLA will serve as a personal guide throughout the course and will serve as the "go-to" person when there's a question or a problem with any of the instruction sessions or weekly assignments. Readers will find SLA questions useful for self-instruction with a coach or mentor. Sample discussion questions for the first week include but are not limited to the following:

- What are your views about power and leadership?
- Who holds the Power of Positive Reputation in your organization?
- What are your major fears? How have you addressed or overcome them?
- What are lessons learned from discovering your dominant, secondary and shadow temperaments?
- What is your dominant temperament?
- What is your shadow temperament and how has it gotten you into trouble?
- What is the dominant temperament of your organization?
- What leadership roles do managers play in your organization?
- How did you decide what you wanted to work on from your Personal Development Challenges?
- What are your strategies for overcoming your three most critical leadership fears?
- What did you learn about yourself as a leader this week?

The following are sample assignments participants will complete by the end of their first program week. Assignments are designed to apply lessons learned from the week's instructional sessions with faculty members back on the job. The successes or remaining tasks of each assignment are discussed at the end of the week with the Strategic Leadership Advisor. Readers may hold these debriefings with coaches or mentors.

Sample Assignments:

1. Read "*What Makes You Tick and What Ticks You Off: How the Basic Elements of Temperament Will Lead You to a Happier Life.*" This is a basic primer on temperament and will aid in further understanding how temperament influences individuals and new leaders.

2. Invite a colleague or coworker who possesses your shadow temperament to a social occasion, such as lunch or coffee. Discuss lessons learned about temperament and ask for insights into how they view the organization, coworkers and colleagues through a temperament lens. Note how their shadow temperament perspectives differ from your own.

3. Consider your secondary temperament and how it influences your dominant temperament. Where is its greatest impact and influence?

4. Give specific examples to justify your assessment of the temperament of your organization.

5. Explore the concept of fear in the workplace and how it may inhibit leadership success.

6. Identify how the leaders in your organization use power.

7. Identify the three most critical issues facing you as a new leader. Be ready to give examples.

8. Identify the personal resources available within your organization to aid and support new leaders (such as people, materials, and budgets.)

9. Review this week's leadership instruction. What made the greatest impact? How might you apply lessons learned on the job?

10. Rate your personal progress in becoming a more effective leader, on a scale of 1 to 10.

The following is a sample checklist that participants may use to track their progress for the week. Checklists are designed to remind participants of tasks that need to be completed during each program week. The checklist may be used to guide debriefings with the Strategic Leadership Advisor. Readers can also use the checklist as a self-assessment tool as they complete various assignments.

Sample Checklist Items:

1. Obtained and read a copy of required book on temperament ☐

2. Identified my dominant and secondary temperaments ☐

3. Reviewed secondary temperament and its influence ☐

4. Completed social interaction with shadow temperament (e.g., coworker, colleague or supervisor) ☐

5. Identified the temperament of my organization ☐

6. Identified my and/or my organization's three most critical leadership issues ☐

7. Found examples of fear in the workplace ☐

8. Identified how organizational leaders use power ☐

9. Identified personal resources on the job ☐

10. Identified most important lessons learned this week ☐

CHAPTER TWO

WEEK 2:
LEADING INDIVIDUALS & TEAMS

The second week of leadership instruction explores a number of critical models and concepts that will help new leaders and managers deal more effectively with individual followers and teams. Readers and live course participants will build upon the knowledge, skills and attitudes developed during the first program week. Key models that are most critical for understanding how to become an effective leader in 30 days include the following:

Situational Leadership®II
The Leadership Challenge
Team Development
Emotional Intelligence
Conflict Management
Servant Leadership

SITUATIONAL LEADERSHIP

According to leadership author John Maxwell, *"The true mea-sure of Leadership is influence—nothing more, nothing less."* So how does the effective leader influence followers? An important model that enables leaders to think about their follower relationships and actually plan their influence on a task-by-task basis is called *Situational Leadership®II* (also known as SLII®).

Developed by Ken Blanchard and the founding associates of The Ken Blanchard Companies, this model has a number of applications that can be immediately applied on the job.

Typically, when a new task or assignment has been identified, the manager or leader will assign the best possible people available. So why doesn't that approach always work? Why don't the best people always complete a task the way the leader wants them to every time? After all, they are our *best people*!

SLII® suggests there's a need to look at a combination of two elements when staffing a new task or assignment. Combined, these elements result in a follower "Development Level." These elements include:

Competence: *the ability, knowledge and skills of the person selected for a particular task; and,*

Commitment: *the self-confidence and self-motivation of the person selected for that particular task.*

The SLII® model encourages the leader to get to know the follower at a deep enough level to enable a determination of his "Development Level"—competence and commitment—and also identifies possible behaviors that can be anticipated at each of four Development Levels.

The four Development Levels are:

Development Level 1 (D1): The individual follower has little or no abilities, knowledge and/or skills in completing the task or assignment. However, he is confident, motivated, and even enthusiastic about doing a good job.

Development Level 2 (D2): The individual follower has some competence in the assigned task. However, commitment is lacking since the difficulties or size of the challenge involved in getting the job done may be perceived as overwhelming.

Development Level 3: (D3): The individual follower has competence in completing the task but still lacks high levels of self-confidence and/or self-motivation.

Development Level 4: (D4): The individual follower has the competence and the commitment to complete the job or assignment as requested.

The effective leader will not provide the same type of leadership approach or style to followers possessing different development levels. The SLII® model provides the leader with four recommended Leadership Styles (S1–S4) matched to each follower's Development Level.

There are four Leadership Styles:

Leadership Style 1 (S1): DIRECTING: The leader provides the D1 follower with very specific direction, supervision, information, and suggestions for completing the task or assignment.

Leadership Style 2 (S2): COACHING: The leader provides the D2 follower with some direction and supervision but also gives support and encouragement to build confidence and to motivate him to take more responsibility.

Leadership Style 3 (S3): SUPPORTING: The leader provides the D3 follower with support and encouragement to build his commitment to the task but offers little direction since the follower is competent in his abilities, knowledge, and skills.

Leadership Style 4 (S4): DELEGATING: The leader provides the D4 follower only with support on an as-needed basis since there is excellence in follower competence and commitment to the task or assignment.

SUMMARY

The SLII® model encourages the effective leader to understand and recognize the competence and commitment of followers. This suggests, much like the Basic Elements® of Temperament, it's often impossible to lead followers using your own preferred leadership style (or dominant temperament). Rather, it's much more effective to use the style that acknowledges follower temperament and development levels.

While it's somewhat obvious that an enthusiastic D1 follower requires specific directions and information about a new task or assignment, other development levels require leaders to be much more aware of both follower skills and attitudes. How do you know when a shift from a coaching leadership style to a supporting style is appropriate? How do you know when a follower is really at the D4 level and not just fooling herself with overconfidence? What about the D3 follower on one task who declares she is at a D4 level on a similar, but new, task? What do you do when you have all four development levels present in one team?

It's incumbent upon leaders to rapidly assess both the competence and commitment of each follower. As leadership trainer and author Glenn Furuya asks, "Is the problem in the skill or the problem in the will?" If it's a *skill* problem, then modeling, practice and feedback are needed to train the follower to an acceptable level of competence. If it's a *will* problem, then a coaching and counseling approach may be best.

However, if author John Maxwell is right and leadership is nothing more than influence, then the effective leader needs to learn how and when to apply personal influence to provide followers with the support they need to become successful in completing a task or assignment. This can mean identifying internal training and development opportunities for new staff members, suggested readings, enrolling followers in workshops or assigning them to shadow more experienced employees to demonstrate an acceptable level of task competence. It also can mean new leaders must reassign followers who have not yet achieved the development level necessary to be successful at a task or assignment.

Situational Leadership®II is a model that addresses both Furuya's and Maxwell's concerns and should be in every leader's toolbox. Additional study of this model will serve as a reminder of the continuing need to understand the competence and commitment of followers.

Ken Blanchard's "Leadership Styles" chart on the following page provides a graphic representation of the interplay between the development level of the individual and the recommended style of leadership needed to insure success.

> *"There's a difference between interest and commitment. When you're interested in doing something, you do it only when it's convenient. When you're committed to something, you accept no excuses—only results."*
>
> —KEN BLANCHARD
> *Coauthor of "Leadership & the One Minute Manager"*

Leadership Styles

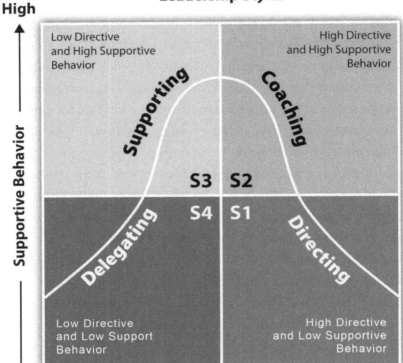

High

Supportive Behavior

Low Directive and High Supportive Behavior

Supporting

High Directive and High Supportive Behavior

Coaching

S3   S2

S4   S1

Delegating

Directing

Low Directive and Low Support Behavior

High Directive and Low Supportive Behavior

Low ——————— **Directive Behavior** ——————→ **High**

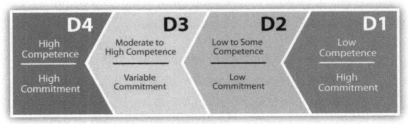

D4	D3	D2	D1
High Competence	Moderate to High Competence	Low to Some Competence	Low Competence
High Commitment	Variable Commitment	Low Commitment	High Commitment

Developed ←——————————— **Developing**

Development Level of the Individual

THE LEADERSHIP CHALLENGE

Another useful model for effective leaders is *The Five Practices of Exemplary Leadership* taken from *The Leadership Challenge®* by authors James Kouzes and Barry Posner. Based on hundreds of thousands of interviews and surveys taken from around the world, this model reads like a checklist for new leaders to measure their progress and success.

There are five leadership practices the authors have found to be critical for leadership success. They include:

Model the Way
Inspire a Shared Vision
Challenge the Process
Enable Others to Act
Encourage the Heart

While many new leaders have some experience and even some expertise in one or more of these exemplary practices, it's the rare leader who has mastered all of them. Let's take a look at each and discuss what they may mean for new leaders and managers.

MODEL THE WAY

This practice asks leaders to serve as role models to their followers. Suggesting that followers, "Do what I say, not what I do," will not result in personal or organizational success, nor will it result in a leader being perceived as effective by followers. "Walking the talk" means one does what one says they'll do, and the result is increased trust, more credibility and an enhanced reputation.

If a leader does not "walk the talk," they'll have a difficult time building trust among followers, and without such trust, virtually any effort on their part to introduce positive change in the organization will face a jaded audience and an uphill battle. How do you increase your ability to *Model the Way*?

- Take whatever steps are necessary to complete personal commitments to others
- Do not make promises that cannot be kept
- Clarify organizational values and act in accordance with them
- Clarify personal values and act in accordance with them
- Look for opportunities to *walk the talk*

Kouzes and Posner say to "Do What You Say You Will Do" and use the acronym DWYSYWD!

INSPIRE A SHARED VISION

This leadership practice is often the most difficult for new leaders to master because it demands a grasp of where their organizations are going and requires some idea as to how to get there. Many new leaders report they're so busy putting out fires, there's rarely enough time to even *think* about the future of their organizations, except during annual strategic planning sessions. Yet this leadership practice is critical for gaining employee buy-in, motivating followers and for aligning the organization towards a successful future.

In order to meet this challenge, new leaders must understand the aspirations of their followers, coworkers, stakeholders, and even clients. Where do members of these groups believe the institution should be headed? What kind of employees will be needed? What skill sets will be developed in-house or contracted out? What changes and/or innovations in products and services will be considered to ensure future competitiveness?

Recall one of the differences between managers and leaders as charted in Chapter One: *Managers see what's going on; leaders see where there is no light and hear when there is no sound.* Inspiring others sometimes means an organization's future is fashioned with little or no information yet in order to enlist others to buy into a vision it needs to be articulated by the leader. Kouzes and Posner suggest you find a common purpose with followers and communicate regularly to learn what they are passionate about. Integrate your own thoughts, feelings and passions about the future of the organization into brief statements and share them with followers and other employees. Insure they recognize their own input in your picture of the company's future. So how do you increase your ability to *Inspire a Shared Vision*?

- Review current strategic plans and other future-oriented documents
- Capture thoughts of key organizational stakeholders about the future of the organization
- Develop a short briefing or "elevator speech" describing an organizational vision
- Share organizational visions with coworkers, stakeholders and clients
- Look for opportunities to share your vision daily

> *"If you keep a clear vision for your future, it will pull you like a magnet through your toughest times."*
>
> —TONY ROBBINS
> *Author & Motivational Speaker*

CHALLENGE THE PROCESS

This practice presents difficulties for many new leaders and managers because it suggests changing the status quo at a time when they're typically trying not to "rock the boat." While leaders are presumed to be role models and quickly demonstrate a capability to articulate an organizational future, they're also expected to generate new ideas and approaches for meeting customer requirements faster and cheaper—all the while using innovative strategies that delineate their organizations from competitors.

Often, new leaders who desire to Challenge the Process complain they don't know how or where to begin. What's needed is a rapid analysis of the organization to identify the 3-5 major processes that impact all or many departments or divisions. A handy tool for getting started is the *Organization as a System* model (see Chapter Three) that partitions the entire organization into quadrants: Social, Strategic, Technical and Administrative. Each sector provides a "big picture" and can help focus on the identification of key processes that overlap or interface with other sectors. Such processes typically include new product development, budgeting, customer service and the procurement of supplies, equipment or materials.

Focus on one to two processes to get started with your analysis. Find a whiteboard and sketch out the process using big rectangles, circles and diamonds to illustrate key activities, yes or no decisions, and other judgment points. Invite coworkers who work on various parts of the process to explain in detail what they do, and have them add more details to the drawing. Those who work within a process are the best ones to improve it. Ask them to specify inhibitors to the process flow. Those are the areas where immediate improvements can occur—the targets to Challenge the Process.

How do you increase your ability to *Challenge the Process*?

- Conduct a rapid organizational analysis using the *Organization as a System* model (see Chapter Three)
- Identify one to two improvement opportunities to focus on first
- Don't be afraid of failure
- Obtain input from various sources (such as followers, coworkers, executives)
- Take limited risks

ENABLE OTHERS TO ACT

New leaders quickly realize they cannot possibly do everything they want to do alone. They'll need the trust and cooperation of followers, employees, coworkers and upper management to support efforts and to execute any innovation. *Teamwork* is a term often used to define the close working relationships between coworkers. In this model, the need for cooperation and trust between the leader and followers is even more important in order to Enable Others to Act.

Developing positive working relationships is crucial to leadership success, as is establishing a working environment conducive to innovation, flexibility, and the generation of ideas. Leaders want followers who'll take personal responsibility, communicate freely, brainstorm creative ideas, and take some levels of risk. Followers will not be able to do that without the support of their leaders and a working climate that encourages them to act as they see fit. So how do you increase your ability *to Enable Others to Act?*

- Build trust with coworkers and other employees
- Ensure that inhibitors to productivity are identified and removed
- Search out opportunities for followers to increase their knowledge and skills
- Identify opportunities to collaborate with followers on a project
- Learn the corporate culture to better understand the working environment, resources, and critical concerns of followers

ENCOURAGE THE HEART

Have you ever worked in an organization where the only time you heard from a leader was during the monthly Friday afternoon party celebrating birthdays? In contrast, effective leaders take every opportunity to recognize followers for their hard work, innovation and customer service. Many followers report all they ever wanted to hear from their leaders was a "thank you" now and then.

Leaders whose goal is to develop positive relationships with their workforce should reward extraordinary individual efforts as well as team success. This exemplary leadership practice implies that the workforce values personal recognition and responds positively to acknowledgment from their leaders. Establishing a working environment that prizes the soliciting, giving and receiving of feedback becomes a major step in the right direction. So how do you increase your ability to successfully *Encourage the Heart?*

- Identify and participate in employee recognition programs
- Learn the first names of followers
- Get out of the office and walk around to greet followers daily
- Analyze any recent employee survey that deals with morale and job satisfaction
- Become personally involved in follower activities

SUMMARY

Authors Kouzes and Posner found after surveying almost 2 million people from around the world that *"those leaders who more frequently use the Five Practices of Exemplary Leadership are considerably more effective than their counterparts who use them infrequently."*

Leadership behavior is of critical importance and concern to new leaders and their followers. Leaders understand they serve as role models. They realize they need to articulate a vision of their organization's future and spread the word. They acknowledge the need to find innovative ways to make their organizations operate more effectively and efficiently. They know they need to establish positive working relationships with followers and build trust. And they need to reward individuals and teams who do extraordinary work and encourage others who need support.

In numerous workshops participants have mentioned to me how they already execute some of these exemplary practices on a regular basis. Many feel they are especially adept at being a role model and rewarding followers for a job well done. That's always good to hear and I always encourage them to work on successfully applying the other exemplary practices as well.

The Five Practices of Exemplary Leadership serve as practical guidelines for new leaders. Each practice is broad enough in concept to encompass a variety of activities and strategies that can result in effective leadership. Especially relevant and helpful during the first year in a new leadership role by virtue of their simplicity and common sense, all five practices can shape your approach and style and serve as a key resource in your journey to becoming an effective leader. This is a resource that deserves a special place in your leadership toolbox.

TASK VS. MAINTENANCE

What do people do that make teams work so successfully? Remember Abraham Maslow's Hierarchy of Needs? He believed individual needs included *Self-Fulfillment* (such as achieving one's potential and being creative*); Psychological* (such as feeling accomplished); and *Basic Needs* (security, safety, food). Individual team members have the same needs as Maslow theorized (e.g., belonging, status, security, self-esteem, and to make a contribution). Teams also have needs. Team needs are divided into Task needs and Maintenance needs. Task and Maintenance needs must be met and, when kept in balance, usually leads to team success.

Task needs include: a clarification and understanding of the problem or task it's working on; a worthwhile and clear goal; a consensus on the goal; a plan of action and procedures; a method for keeping on course; and an acknowledgement of accomplishment.

Maintenance needs include: improving team understanding of the problem or task; enhancing team communication; achieving a sense of team unity; experiencing a sense of sharing; and developing an *"esprit de corps."*

Have you ever been on a team that did a great job in completing its task or solving a problem but you hated every minute you served on it? That means the Task vs. Maintenance balance was tilted too strongly toward accomplishing tasks to the detriment of positive working relationships. In the short-term, bottom-line, focus of most businesses today, it is all too common for teams to have a task bias.

If you've ever been on a team that didn't get the job done but you enjoyed every minute you were on it, you've experienced a tilt toward maintenance to the detriment of completing the task. A team that fails to achieve its goal will soon be disbanded.

The job of a team leader is to insure that efforts to balance the achievement of Task and Maintenance needs are planned and executed. Today, many effective leaders call a halt to all tasks with 5-10 minutes left in their session to touch on maintenance issues. Often all it takes is a leader asking the team to reflect for a moment on their working relationships, the effectiveness of their communication, their continued understanding of the task at hand, and whether there are any individual issues that the team should know about. Comments can begin a conversation that may lead to additional problem clarification, improvements in team processes and procedures, and a strengthening of the team bond.

STAGES OF TEAM DEVELOPMENT

Author Bruce Tuckman, in 1965, developed a model that tracked and predicted the progression of group and team development that has become a critical addition for the toolboxes of every new leader and manager. When leading teams, or even when serving as a team member, it's important to understand the group's progress through a number of predictable stages. This aids the leader in understanding and explaining team member behavior, especially disagreements or arguments that tend to last much longer than perhaps they should. Tuckman designed a four-stage model and then revised it in 1977 to add a fifth stage (Adjourning).

STAGE 1: FORMING

Tuckman viewed this stage as one of "testing." New team members become oriented to their roles, tasks, and operating processes (a task and interpersonal domain focus), which test their abilities to be heard by the group and to provide input into decision-making. They experience dependent relationships with team leaders, and the Task vs. Maintenance balance is tilted toward Task.

STAGE 2: STORMING

This second stage of team development is characterized by conflict and emotional responses to tasks and interpersonal relationships. There's typically resistance to team procedures and the requirements of team tasks. This is a critical stage for many teams who often fail to ever emerge from it and disband. The Task vs. Maintenance balance is tilted toward Maintenance since team leaders are typically working to enhance communication, reduce conflicts and insure goal alignment and team consensus.

STAGE 3: NORMING

The third stage heralds the overcoming of resistance and the return of team cohesiveness. Often, new roles or operating processes and procedures are adopted. Sometimes leadership is changed or rotated to other team members. Sometimes sub-teams are formed to address a particular portion of the larger task. Team members are able to express personal opinions to each other without fear of criticism. The Task vs. Maintenance balance is nearly equal, with Task typically still more pronounced since the team has emerged from its storming stage and is once again focused on achieving its goals.

STAGE 4: PERFORMING

The fourth stage of team development finds members functioning effectively and flexibly as they focus on completing all remaining aspects of their task. All structural questions involving roles, processes and procedures are resolved, and the nature of team working relationships becomes the major strength for accomplishing job goals. The Task vs. Maintenance balance is equal; with the team recognizing their interpersonal success has aided them in completing their tasks in an effective and efficient manner.

STAGE 5: ADJOURNING

The final stage involves the completing of team tasks and the dissolution of the team or group. If unplanned, a "mourning" feeling for members is not unusual, especially when a team is disbanded without warning. In such cases, members regret their experience could not end on a more positive and happier note. Often, the adjourning stage ends with a celebration and/or party; an acknowledgement of a job well done by upper management;

and, expectations for working together again on future projects. Members feel satisfied with their team experience and thankful for the lasting friendships made.

TUCKMAN'S STAGES OF TEAM DEVELOPMENT

TEAM STAGE	TASKS	BEHAVIORS
FORMING (STAGE 1)	Establishing expectations. Agreeing on goals. Developing operating procedures.	Developing trust. Making initial contacts. Members are dependent on the team leader for information and guidance.
STORMING (STAGE 2)	Dealing with power and control issues. Members strive to articulate issues of concerns (such as leadership, goals and processes).	Expressing differences of opinions & feelings. Negative reaction to leadership decisions. Members are independent or counter-dependent.
NORMING (STAGE 3)	Agreeing on roles, operating procedures and decision-making. Operating effectively.	Decision are made using consensus and negotiation. Members agree on personal responsibilities.
PERFORMING (STAGE 4)	Achieving effective goals. Completing assignment on time.	Members collaborate. "Esprit de Corps" established. Members are empathetic. Members know what to do without being told.
ADJOURNING (STAGE 5)	Dissolution of team or group. Termination of roles. Completion of tasks. Acknowledgement of team effort.	"Mourning" or loss by team members, especially if Stage 5 is a surprise or unplanned. Gratitude by members.

A better understanding of this model equips the new leader with a template for identifying the progress of a team or group. It's often the case in organizations that several teams are operating simultaneously at different stages. One team may be bogged down in Storming Stage 2 while another team is in Performing Stage 4.

One also can make the case the team stage in the Tuckman model has the same characteristics as the development level of individuals in *Situational Leadership®II*. For example:

Situational Leadership®II	Tuckman
(D1): Low Competence/High Commitment	FORMING (STAGE 1)
(D2): Some Competence/Low Commitment	STORMING (STAGE 2)
(D3): High Competence/Variable Commitment	NORMING (STAGE 3)
(D4): High Competence/High Commitment	PERFORMING (STAGE 4)

SUMMARY

A unique aspect of the Tuckman model is that when a "Performing" team is assigned a new task, or if a new member joins the group, the entire team reverts back to "Forming." This serves as a warning to teams and organizations with new hires who come on board with virtually no orientation or assistance and then are criticized for taking too long to "catch on" or "catch up."

The Tuckman model is a tool for any leader to make a quick assessment of the development stage of a work team, task force or committee. Each stage builds upon the previous one. The model is also useful for helping team members discern personal problems and concerns with their team experience. It's common for an organization to have several teams at different stages of development at the same time. This requires leaders to understand the model and take necessary actions to support and guide each team toward success. The Tuckman model is a helpful leadership tool that needs to be in the toolbox of every new leader and manager.

EMOTIONAL INTELLIGENCE

How do we know what makes a good leader? Thus far, a number of models have guided your understanding and analysis of individual and team behaviors, but is having these models in your leadership toolbox enough for you to become successful? Psychologist Daniel Goleman set out to learn why some leaders are so effective while others are not—even those with superior intelligence and highly developed technical skills.

Goleman studied more than 180 U.S. and international organizations (such as British Air, Lucent, and Credit Suisse) and found the personal styles of leaders differed markedly. Some were analytical, some were subdued and shy, some were fiery, and some were moody and situational. He found that although many leaders possessed great technical abilities, their employees often rated them poorly; other leaders held superior cognitive abilities and long-term vision for their organizations yet were still rated poorly. Some leaders, however, who were perhaps not as intelligent or skilled, were rated very high. Why such differences?

According to Goleman, the difference between an effective leader and a poor leader was their Emotional Intelligence or EI (or EQ), for short. He defined this crucial personal asset as:

> *"The capacity for recognizing our own feelings and those of others, for motivating ourselves, for managing emotions well in ourselves and in our relationships."*

Those surveyed leaders who demonstrated Emotional Intelligence were rated much higher than those who did not—no matter their backgrounds, intelligence or skill levels. The most effective leaders shared one characteristic: they possessed Emotional Intelligence. New leaders find there are many emotions swirling around the workplace at any given moment, and they'll no doubt encounter one or more of them daily. A workplace behavior or offhanded remark from a follower, coworker or manager may result in touching a personal "hot button," and trigger a negative emotional reaction.

For example, a leader with an Earth shadow temperament is abruptly told by a dominant Earth executive she *must* turn in a report on time or face the consequences. This "threat" triggers a negative knee-jerk reaction from the leader—in other words, it touches her hot button! A typical reaction when a hot button is touched is the *"fight or flight"* response. In this example, the leader may snap back a pointed barb at the executive, saying in very plain and pointed language she knows her job and what's expected and doesn't need anyone telling her what to do or how to do it! Another response may be for her to say nothing while actually seething with anger inside. She then adds this Earth executive to her list of *persona non grata*.

Confronting or avoiding a supervisor who touches a hot button are not ideal leadership approaches and can result in arguments, hurt feelings, internal strife, loss of integrity and a negative mark against personal reputations. Goleman originally developed the EI model to shed light on how to recognize and manage personal emotions. His efforts have been revised into today's *Emotional and Social Intelligence in Leadership* model. This new model suggests a better, more effective way of dealing with the emotions that often surface in workplace situations and can lead to dysfunction and long-term strife. The model includes 12 competencies that increase EI levels with each step.

EMOTIONAL AND SOCIAL INTELLIGENCE IN LEADERSHIP

SELF-AWARENESS

In the earlier example, the dominant Earth executive (the new leader's shadow temperament) has hit her hot button. Instead of reacting with the fight or flight response, which has many potentially negative consequences, Emotional Intelligence (EI) reminds the new leader to recognize and understand her emotional reaction to the situation.

Emotional Self-Awareness: Leaders with high EI acknowledge and can articulate how a hot button statement or behavior from a supervisor (or anyone else, for that matter) can be internalized as hurtful, demeaning, and mean-spirited. Knowing and understanding one's normal reaction to such statements, however, can prepare and enable leaders to stay true to their values without endangering their role and/or positions in the organization.

SELF-MANAGEMENT

Building on the Self-Awareness competency above, leaders are reminded that jumping to conclusions (see the Results-Model in Chapter Four) without learning what intentions lay behind a hot button comment or behavior may trigger a strong negative reaction that could be completely unfounded. In the earlier example, the executive may have been reprimanded himself by the company's president for untimely reporting of information and then took out his anger on the new leader.

> *Emotional Self-Control:* When faced with an emotional situation, leaders with high EI carve out time to relax, take a deep breath and ask themselves questions to keep their emotions in check. Questions help clarify

situations (What's really the issue here? What Mental Map am I using in this situation and has it been updated?) Questions help to delay knee-jerk reactions that can get one into trouble.

Achievement Oriented: Leaders recognize how the management of emotions, especially during stressful situations, aids in improving leadership performance and avoiding conflicts. Skills are used to work effectively toward goal achievement rather than trying to "get even" with someone who touched a hot button.

Positive Outlook: This competency encompasses how the leader views the world, organization and other people. Personal temperament is a major influence in developing and maintaining a positive view of followers as well as the institution (see Basic Elements of Temperament in Chapter One.) A positive outlook also can reduce the negative impact that accompanies a violation of personal values and/or the touching of a hot button.

Adaptability: Over time, leaders with high EI become more comfortable during uncomfortable situations and in recognizing the need to remain flexible in dealing with emotional issues and situations. Experienced leaders are great sources of knowledge for advising new leaders how to deal effectively with workplace issues that can cause emotional distress.

SOCIAL AWARENESS

Building on the cumulative achievements from Self-Awareness and Self-Management competencies, the EI leader demonstrates an awareness and understanding of personal emotions and those of others. In the earlier hot button example, leaders at this EI competency level are better able to understand the emotional state of the dominant Earth executive who triggered the hot button. They can observe and understand nonverbal communication and/or other physical manifestations and persevere in efforts to attain additional insight into what makes people tick.

> *Empathy:* One of the most critical aspects of this leadership model, the *Empathy* competency, provides skill in viewing followers, colleagues, and coworkers as internal clients or customers and discerning their emotional makeup. This assists the EI leader in developing (and retaining) a more skilled and diverse workforce and enhancing customer service by being more sensitive to client needs and emotions.

> *Organizational Awareness:* A critical aspect of *Social Awareness* is an enhanced appreciation and skill in understanding how organizations operate. The EI leader knows how and where power is distributed and who holds formal and informal power (see Types of Power in Chapter One). Leaders are skilled in developing relationships that will help them increase their personal networks that serve as resources and support for on-the-job guidance and for ensuring that company values are maintained.

RELATIONSHIP MANAGEMENT

At this level, EI leaders combine all previous competencies and are aware of the need to establish and maintain positive working relationships at all organizational levels. They also understand the benefits of establishing critically important professional networks. EI leaders are instrumental in efforts to lead organizational change and are adept at developing and managing teams to achieve work tasks and achieve goals.

Influence: EI leaders are skilled in the art of persuasion at virtually all levels in the workplace. They can easily establish rapport and exert influence with individuals and groups to accept change (see Influencing Organizational Change in Chapter Three). They're team-builders and have little difficulty in forming working groups and teams, often because followers wish to work with them. EI leaders at this level have gained the respect of the workforce.

Coach and Mentor: EI leaders recognize the importance of developing and supporting a skilled workforce, whether they take the forms of teams, committees, task forces or individuals. They're aware of the skills and abilities of employees and can identify the bureaucratic roadblocks faced daily by their followers. Leaders are adept at asking for, giving and receiving feedback, especially in terms of assessing the competence and commitment of employees. EI leaders are often sought after as coaches or mentors to other leaders, followers, and coworkers and spend additional time supporting and encouraging others.

Conflict Management: This competency equips EI leaders with skills to deal effectively with conflict (see Conflict Management in Chapter Two) and resistance to change. Leaders are skilled at generating solutions to conflicts by finding common ground, listening and seeking the opinions of all players.

Inspirational Leadership: The ability to influence others and resolve conflicts assists the EI leader in articulating a vision of the organization's future and persuading others to accept and support that vision. The EI leader also is skilled at pointing out, to followers and coworkers, the purpose of their work and how it fits into the greater corporate picture (see The Leadership Challenge in Chapter Two). Inspiring others is often the most contentious competency for a new leader to acquire and requires time, effort and organizational knowledge to master.

Teamwork: The EI leader is the consummate team player. Personal involvement and commitment are instrumental in establishing a respectful working environment conducive to cooperation and group effort. It also includes influencing followers, coworkers and colleagues to become more involved and supportive of various team and group activities as well as over-arching institutional goals.

SUMMARY

Daniel Goleman's Emotional and Social Intelligence in Leadership model provides new leaders with a competency-based approach for becoming more effective in dealing with personal emotions and the emotions of others. Increasing EI skills with each step, EI competencies are broad and encompass a variety of behaviors ranging from self-awareness to networking to managing organizational relationships.

Some believe the only skill a leader really needs is Emotional Intelligence. The ability to remain calm while others flail around is a critical skill and pays off with positive perceptions by followers and supervisors alike. Emotional Intelligence is a skill that can trouble the new leader because it's difficult to self-evaluate when seemingly caught in the midst of an emotional situation (see Results-Model in Chapter Four).

Combined with studies on temperament, conflict management, power, influence and decision-making, Goleman's model offers a plethora of opportunities to expand personal knowledge of emotions, management, self-awareness, workforce relationships, and, most of all, leadership.

> *"But once you are in the field, Emotional Intelligence emerges as a much stronger predictor of who will be most successful, because it is how we handle ourselves in our relationships that determine how well we do once we are in a given job."*
>
> —DANIEL GOLEMAN
> *Author & Psychologist*

EMOTIONAL & SOCIAL INTELLIGENCE IN LEADERSHIP

STAGE	DEFINITION	HALLMARKS
SELF-AWARENESS	The ability to recognize and understand moods, emotions, & drives, as well as their effect on others	Self-Confidence Realistic self-assessment Self-deprecating sense of humor
EMOTIONAL SELF-AWARENESS	Attuned to feelings and their impact on job performance	Willingness to speak about emotions Values-based decision-making

STAGE	DEFINITION	HALLMARKS
SELF-MANAGEMENT	The ability to control or redirect disruptive impulses/moods; the propensity to suspend judgment and think before acting	Trustworthiness and integrity Comfort with ambiguity Openness to change
EMOTIONAL SELF-CONTROL	Skill in managing personal emotions	Remaining calm in stressful situations Clear thinking Keeping an emotional balance
ACHIEVEMENT ORIENTATION	Holding oneself and others to high standards	Seeking improved performance Working toward challenging and measurable goals
POSITIVE OUTLOOK	Viewing every situation as an opportunity	Seeing others in a positive light Expecting future changes to be positive
ADAPTABILITY	Ability to handle many demands while maintaining focus on organizational goals	Comfortable with uncertainty Flexible when handling change
SOCIAL AWARENESS	A passion to work for reasons that go beyond money or status; a propensity to pursue goals with energy and persistence	Strong drive to achieve Optimism even in the face of failure Organizational commitment

STAGE	DEFINITION	HALLMARKS
EMPATHY	Understanding the emotional makeup of other people; skill in treating people according to their emotional reactions	Expertise in building/ retaining talent Cross-cultural sensitivity Service to clients and customers
ORGANIZATIONAL AWARENESS	Understanding of all organizational components and aspects	Identifying formal and informal power sources Aware of relationships for networking, guidance, and values
RELATIONSHIP MANAGEMENT	Proficiency in managing relationships and building networks; ability to find common ground and build rapport	Effectiveness in leading change Persuasiveness Expertise in building and leading teams
INFLUENCE	Ability to appeal to others & attain buy-in	Persuasive with individuals and groups
COACH & MENTOR	Taking active interest in assisting others in the use of formal and informal methods	Recognizing strengths and challenges of workforce Providing feedback Aiding in growth opportunities
CONFLICT MANAGEMENT	Making an effort to understand different perspectives	Assisting in finding common ground Seeking everyone's opinions Working toward finding solutions

STAGE	DEFINITION	HALLMARKS
INSPIRATIONAL LEADERSHIP	Ability to show others the purpose of their day-to-day work	Articulating a future vision Succeeding at having people join them
TEAMWORK	Aid teams in developing an identity, positive relationships, and spirit	Helping others commit to group efforts Building an atmosphere of cooperation, helpfulness and respect

"If your emotional abilities aren't in hand, if you don't have self-awareness, if you are not able to manage your distressing emotions, if you can't have empathy and have effective relationships, then no matter how smart you are, you are not going to get very far."

—DANIEL GOLEMAN
Author & Psychologist

CONFLICT MANAGEMENT

Author Warren Bennis posits that today's organizations need leaders who are equipped with three key skills:

1. An ability to enlist others and motivate them to seek resolution to conflict;
2. A capacity to exercise good judgment; and,
3. An orientation to respect others.

Authors Kenneth Cloke and Joan Goldsmith, in *"Resolving Conflicts at Work: Ten Strategies for Everyone On The Job,"* point out most of what we know about conflict resolution comes from what we learned in our childhood—and that's not very much!

Lacking conflict management skills, a first response at work is often to avoid or suppress conflict, thereby cheating the leader, the other party and the organization out of learning about real core problems and how to prevent them in the future. Institutions, according to Cloke and Goldsmith, also tend to sweep conflicts "under the rug," actually rewarding employees for avoiding conflicts.

Remember that your shadow temperament may be at the source of your conflict with a follower, colleague, manager or client (see Basic Elements of Temperament in Chapter One). As your least preferred behavior, your shadow can influence your perception of a situation and your reaction to it. Your Mental Map (see Results-Model in Chapter Four), created by experiences, temperament, beliefs, values, culture, education and other factors resides in your head and thrusts itself into action when you run into any event—or conflict.

Let's look at Cloke and Goldsmith's 10 strategies to address conflict:

1. *Understand the Culture and Dynamics of Conflict:* Since conflict implies a "rupture in the culture," one must be aware of how organizational culture looks at conflict. Is it acceptable? What are the rules? In the United States, conflicts in the movies and television are not typically resolved with mediation, negotiating or other methods but rather with violence. Listening and thoughtfulness are depicted as boring, naïve or cowardly. Aggression is typically presented as a passionate and justified conflict resolution tactic. So if organizational leaders look to popular culture for how to resolve conflicts, they won't get much help.

2. *Listen Empathetically and Responsively:* To be more effective communicators in conflict situations, new leaders must: 1) examine their words, tone, body language and metaphors that can convey true meaning to the listener; 2) examine how respectfully, empathetically and responsively messages are being sent and received; and, 3) examine personal relationships with the speaker, including unspoken interests, needs, emotions and expectations.

3. *Search Beneath the Surface for Hidden Meanings:* Think of an iceberg. Most of its mass lies hidden from sight with only a small percentage sticking up for all to see. Think of conflicts the same way. The presenting problem may only be a small portion of a complex and long simmering set of issues.

4. *Acknowledge and Reframe Emotions:* As in the study of *Emotional Intelligence* and temperament, workplace emotions can play a crucial role in conflict management. Often, the leader's inability to deal with personal emotions limits her capacity to empathize with the emotions of others. "Reframing" requires changing an accusation ("You sound like an idiot!") to an "I" statement ("What did I do to make you say that?").

5. *Separate What Matters from What Gets in the Way:* Instead of thinking the leader holds the only "truth" in a conflict, reflect that there are usually multiple truths. Focus on the issues themselves and separate them from the individual or group that brings them up.

6. *Solve Problems Paradoxically and Creatively:* Be collaborative in solving the conflict and realize there may be more than one solution, and that potential solutions may contradict each other.

7. *Learn from Difficult Behaviors:* Reframe the conflict from being a difficult "problem" or "person" to a "behavior" or "relationship." This prevents blaming the individual for the problem and encourages viewing it as an opportunity to practice awareness and empathy.

8. *Lead and Coach for Transformation:* This strategy links back to previous discussions on power, integrity and *The Five Practices of Exemplary Leadership.* The ability to be self-aware and to communicate a future vision for the organization enables leaders to create working environments where followers are encouraged to ask questions, invite discussion, and surface their personal concerns.

9. *Explore Resistance and Negotiate Collaboratively:* This strategy is a reminder that collaboration, where the interests of both sides of a conflict are satisfied, typically works best. Resistance to proposed solutions is often linked to organizational change and should not be discounted as simply stubbornness.

10. *Mediate and Design Systems for Preventions:* A survey by the American Management Association (AMA) of CEOs, VPs, and middle managers revealed they were spending at least 24 percent of their time resolving conflicts. Designing and establishing an internal mediation system acknowledges that "conflict" is a system requiring analysis and tracking over time. Experienced mediators often reach agreements in less than half a day and resolve an average of 80-95 percent of conflicts they address.

"Every conflict reflects what each person most needs to learn in that moment."

—KENNETH CLOKE
Coauthor of "Resolving Conflicts at Work"

TKI CONFLICT MODE INSTRUMENT

A conflict management model proven to be useful to new leaders is the *Thomas-Kilmann Conflict Mode Instrument*, better known as the TKI. Developed by Kenneth Thomas and Ralph Kilmann, this model identifies five responses to conflict and views them as strategies on an axis between high and low levels of assertiveness and cooperativeness:

Avoiding: Low Assertiveness/Low Cooperativeness. An individual does not pursue either her or her opponent's concerns. She does not address the conflict.

Accommodating: Low Assertiveness/High Cooperativeness. An individual's main concern is to satisfy the opponent's concerns at the expense of her own.

Competing: High Assertiveness/Low Cooperativeness. An individual pursues her own interests at the expense of the opponent using whatever power she has available.

Compromising: Assertive/Cooperative. Both the individual and opponent give up half their interests in order to reach a mutually acceptable solution.

Collaborating: High Assertiveness/High Cooperativeness. An individual tries to work with her opponent to find a mutually satisfying solution. It may require analyzing concerns and finding a number of potential alternatives.

Authors Thomas and Kilmann posit that leaders repeatedly use one or two conflict management styles as virtual default approaches no matter the type of conflict and suggest new leaders develop all five styles to be better able to handle all types of conflict situations.

CONFLICT MANAGEMENT STYLES

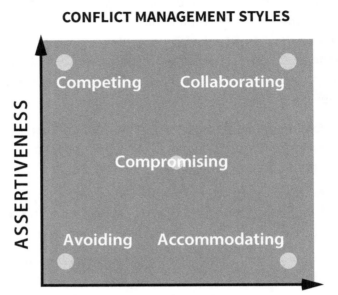

Exhibit 1: Overview of TKI Conflict Mode Instrument. Copyright © 2009–2017 by Kilmann Diagnostics. All rights reserved. Original figure is available at: http://www.kilmanndiagnostics.com/overview-thomas-kilmann-conflict-mode-instrument-tki

Authors Kenneth Cloke and Joan Goldsmith view the *TKI Conflict Mode Instrument* as strategies that differentiate the concern for people versus the concern for results:

> **Avoiding:** Low Relationship/Low Results. An individual has a low need for maintaining a relationship with an opponent and a low concern for achieving a solution to the conflict.

Accommodating: High Relationship/Low Results. An individual has a high need for maintaining a relationship with an opponent and a low concern for achieving a solution to the conflict.

Competing: Low Relationship/High Results. An individual has a low need to maintain the relationship with an opponent and a high concern for achieving a solution to the conflict.

Compromising: Maintaining Relationship/Achieving Results. An individual has a need for maintaining a relationship with an opponent and a concern for achieving a solution to the conflict.

Collaborating: High Relationship/High Results. An individual has a high need for maintaining a relationship with an opponent and a high concern for achieving a solution to the conflict.

SUMMARY

As a new leader or manager, effectively handling conflicts can be time-consuming and at times heartbreaking. These models provide insight for a range of short and long-term approaches—from immediate conflict-handling behaviors and the development of an open and positive working environment to the establishment of conflict management systems.

As Cloke and Goldsmith state, *"A skillful person is able to employ each (Conflict Management) response at the right moment, with the right person, to solve the right problem in the right way."*

As readers explore more literature on conflict management and the models designed to assist in the handling of this often-disagreeable task (see Reference Section), they'll begin to form personal opinions about their preferences for managing conflicts. Feel free to borrow from all models, and don't get caught in the trap of addressing conflicts the same way every time.

> *"Everything that irritates us about others can lead us to an understanding of ourselves."*
>
> —CARL JUNG
> *Swiss Psychiatrist & Psychoanalyst*

SERVANT LEADERSHIP

A final leadership model to consider when dealing with individuals and organizations is very popular with readers today, *Servant Leadership*. Several books have been written on the topic although the original concept began in the 1960s with the late philosopher and author Robert Greenleaf.

Greenleaf's basic idea was that followers who view their leaders as *servants* are much more productive than those who perceive their leaders as enforcers with Position Power (see Types of Power in Chapter One). Servant-leaders are continually listening, exploring, giving and receiving feedback, and strategizing ways to make organizations better.

Greenleaf wrote that General George Washington signed his letters, "Your most humble and obedient servant," and asks, "Would anyone say George Washington was not an effective leader?" As a general and leader of the American Revolution, Washington could be considered an individual with considerable Position Power. Yet he viewed himself as a servant-leader.

Greenleaf believed the concept of "leader-first" and "servant-first" are polar extremes. The motivation of the "leader-first" is to embody Position Power, authority and enforcement, whereas the "servant-first" leader is motivated by the need to meet the highest priorities of followers. There are direct overlaps between the servant-first leader and the dominant Water temperament, whose highest values also focus on the development, care and benefit of others.

The servant-leader asks, "There is an organizational problem, so what can I do about it?" The leader-first (using her Position Power authority) asks, "There is an organizational problem, so who should I get to solve it for me?" Given these differing viewpoints, the servant-leader uses active listening, feedback, intuition and empathy, and seeks follower input so he can take the lead in solving the problem or solving it personally. The leader-first may use these same methods but her purpose is to identify the best follower or team to take the lead for solving the problem.

Servant Leaders value the development of trust with followers who they view as internal customers. They keep their ears to the ground and have established communication networks that keep them abreast of corporate issues that they may personally address on behalf of their followers. They understand follower concerns and continually strive to locate and obtain the resources needed to address those concerns.

Leader-first practitioners often view followers as a labor force whose responsibilities are mainly to take orders and complete assignments without complaint or resistance. They are apt to be perceived by followers as part of an elite management or executive team that shares the bare minimum of information and are often clueless about key follower concerns or issues. They are reactionary in their approach by scrambling the workforce, often at a moment's notice, to locate the oilcan to lubricate the squeakiest organizational wheel.

"The essential quality that sets servant-leaders apart from others is that they live by their conscience—the inward moral sense of what is right and what is wrong."

—STEPHEN COVEY

Author of "The 7 Habits of Highly Effective People"

Author Stephen Covey goes on to say that the moral guidelines of Servant Leaders are actually a set of universal truths or values all cultures, races and religions share: fairness, honesty, respect and contribution. These values mesh with international surveys conducted by Kouzes and Posner that indicate honesty (88 percent of respondents) and competence (66 percent) are key characteristics of successful leaders.

SUMMARY

New leaders have a choice to make as they deeply examine their personal motivations for accepting positions that promote them up their corporate hierarchies and chains of command: leader-first or servant-first? Is their key motivation one of assuming the positional power and its attendant desirability and prestige they may have sought throughout their careers, or is it one of service to others?

Robert Greenleaf said leaders are better than others at pointing a path to the future and have the ability to articulate that future to others. This implies such leaders have a degree of intuition and inspiration to step out in front of the pack and ask others to follow them. Followers will not support a leader they neither trust, nor one to whom they do not relate in terms of their values, honesty, competency and commitment.

Servant-leaders know their followers well. They know their strengths and they know their inhibitions and frustrations. They know what makes them tick. They know to succeed they must demonstrate a commitment to serving the needs of their followers. That doesn't mean carrying out every idea, plan, strategy, product, or service improvement that's suggested or recommended; it means empathizing with each individual and accepting their contribution and input as viable attempts to strengthen their organizations.

Servant leadership also is consistent with the philosophy of Ken Blanchard in *Situational Leadership®II*. Doesn't it make sense that in order to assess levels of follower competency and commitment to a particular task or assignment, leaders must know their followers well? They must know their strengths and skill gaps. They must know what motivates them. Servant-leaders will do what it takes to support the efforts of their followers to gain skills, knowledge and improve attitudes.

Servant leadership also is consistent with *The Five Practices of Exemplary Leadership*. "Enabling Others to Act" and "Encourage the Heart" require leaders to know their followers and provide the necessary knowledge, skills and inspiration to make them successful.

Servant Leadership, *Situational Leadership®II*, Emotional Intelligence and *The Five Practices of Exemplary Leadership* all require a degree of understanding and empathy by the leaders who utilize these popular and useful approaches to leadership.

> *"Servant-leadership is more than a concept, it is a fact. Any great leader, by which I also mean an ethical leader of any group, will see herself or himself as a servant of that group and will act accordingly."*
>
> —M. SCOTT PECK
> *Author of "The Road Less Travelled"*

At the end of the second week of live instruction, course participants meet again with their Strategic Leadership Advisor (SLA) by phone or online. It's anticipated that participants may have more specific questions about leadership as their knowledge expands and their experience in applying leadership models and concepts on the job broadens. Readers will find the SLA questions below useful for self-instruction and conversations with coaches and mentors.

- How does your organization assess employee competence and commitment?
- How have you dealt with followers who have low competence in a task but high commitment and a strong willingness to try?
- In which of *The Five Practices of Exemplary Leadership* do you feel most skilled and confident? Least?
- What has been your experience in *Modeling the Way*? What techniques have you used and what was the reaction of followers?
- What stage of development is your team, branch or division?
- What are the key processes in your organization? How will you go about challenging them?
- How will you establish trust with your followers?
- What has been your experience with *Emotional Intelligence*? What is your reaction to its competencies?
- How have you provided "support" to followers without micromanaging them?

- What are the advantages of servant-first leadership styles? Leader-first?

- Describe your success in addressing your three most critical leadership concerns. How have they changed as you have tried to address them?

- What did you learn about yourself as a leader this week?

The following are sample assignments course participants complete by the end of the second program week. Assignments are designed to apply lessons learned from the week's live instructional sessions with faculty members on the job. The successes or remaining tasks of each assignment are discussed at the end of the week with the Strategic Leadership Advisor. Readers also can complete these assignments and debrief their experiences with a coach or mentor.

Sample Assignments:

1. Interview several of your organizational leaders to learn how they diagnose the competence and commitment of followers to complete a task. How do they know their assessments are accurate?

2. Consider how your earlier study of temperament links to *Situational Leadership®II*. Are they complementary?

3. Identify how you might utilize *Situational Leadership®II* styles in your everyday role as a new leader.

4. Identify examples of leaders in your organization modeling the way. What behaviors are they employing?

5. Assess your team, branch, or division. What behaviors are being exhibited? What is their stage of development?

6. How have you used *Emotional Intelligence* on the job? Give examples.

7. Be ready to give examples of how conflicts are handled in your organization.

8. Identify opportunities your organization offers employees to enhance personal skills and abilities.

9. Review this week's leadership instruction. What made the greatest impact on you? How might you apply what you learned on the job?

10. Be ready to discuss how you rate your progress in becoming an effective leader.

WEEK 2 QUICK CHECKLIST

The following is a sample checklist participants may be asked to complete by their second program week. Checklists are designed to remind participants of work that needs to be done during the week and provides a method for keeping track of their progress. The checklist may be reviewed and discussed at the end of the week with the Strategic Leadership Advisor, coach, or mentor. Readers also can use the checklist as a self-instruction tool as you complete various assignments.

Sample Checklist Items:

1. Identify your leaders' methods of diagnosing employee competence and commitment. ☐
2. Identify leaders who "Model the Way". ☐
3. Practice Situational Leadership approaches. ☐
4. Diagnose a follower's competence and commitment. ☐
5. Link temperament to Situational Leadership. ☐
6. Consider how to utilize *Emotional Intelligence* on the job. ☐
7. Identify overlaps between leadership and management. ☐
8. Identify conflict management approaches. ☐
9. Identify stage of team/branch development. ☐
10. Identify personal resources on the job. ☐
11. Identify most important lessons learned this week. ☐
12. Rate your leadership progress this week (scale of 1–10). ☐

CHAPTER THREE

WEEK 3:
LEADING ORGANIZATIONS

During the third week of leadership instruction, readers and live course participants explore several models and concepts that focus on operating dynamically as a leader in the organization. Key models that are most critical for understanding how to become an effective leader in 30 days include the following:

Organization Culture

Organization as a System Model

Influencing Organizational Change

Asking Effective Questions

Thus far, readers and participants have reflected on how they'll lead themselves and how to lead individuals and teams. Many new leaders have even greater responsibilities for the management of branches, divisions, departments, and even entire organizations. Will the same techniques work for larger groups that worked well for you with smaller teams and individuals? How should one prepare for such responsibilities?

What is an Organization?

The Merriam-Webster dictionary defines an organization as, "An administrative and functional structure (as a business or a political party)." Another definition is, "An organized body of people with a particular purpose, especially in business, society, association, etc."

New leaders often are unsure of their scopes of work and spheres of influence. How many levels down does a leader's scope include? To what extent does a leader have direct authority over employees from other departments or divisions? What responsibility and influence does a new leader have when examining the corporate chain of command?

All these questions need to be answered, and it's the responsibility of the new leader to find those answers. Some answers may, indeed, be found in a policy, company handbook or job description (although they're often dated and frequently irrelevant) while others will be communicated directly by executives or supervisors. Many, however, are discerned only through experience. The job of a new leader or manager, especially in an organization that is new to them, is to know where to look.

One of the first places to understand what makes an organization tick is its administrative and functional structure. Is it more traditionally hierarchical or "tall" and headed by a chief executive officer (CEO), a director or a president? Or is it a more modern, flat organization with few administrative levels, led by a board or executive committee who report to a director or chairperson?

A more traditional organization often means leaders are assigned to head specific sub-groups (such as branches, divisions, or departments) with no other authority, whereas matrixes or flatter organizations may require much broader spheres of authority across departmental lines. There are many examples where leaders only see their direct reports in a matrix organization once a year during performance reviews and must rely on others to actually evaluate their own followers.

Exhibit 2: Flat vs. Tall Organizational Hierarchy
Tall Organizational Structure

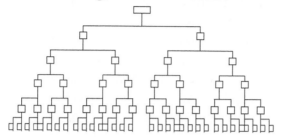

Flat Organizational Structure

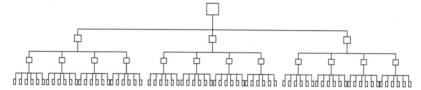

ORGANIZATIONAL CULTURE

Another avenue for new leaders to learn and explore their organizations is through a better understanding of corporate culture. When a new hire first enters an organization, how does she learn how things operate? Sometimes there are policy manuals that show all the rules; organizational charts depicting reporting relationships; and, strategic plans, mission statements and vision statements showing future directions. Perhaps there are other corporate documents to acquaint the newcomer with operational policies, procedures and practices. If one is lucky, some poor soul is "volun-told" (told to volunteer) to help the newcomer by "showing them the ropes." But just what are the ropes and how does one get a feel for what really goes on after the orientation ends?

Organizational Culture (also called Corporate Culture) refers to those behaviors, attitudes and beliefs that have been developed over time and are valued by employees and the institution. Such values and beliefs may be written in the form of an operating manual or as a slogan on the wall but are more often unwritten. Imagine, the most critical rules all employees abide by and reflect the self-image of the organization are typically unwritten!

Chapter One asked, "Do you know of an organization that's perceived by customers, employees and the public as living its culture?" A number of companies were mentioned. Southwest Airlines was listed for communicating its vision to employees who are authorized at the lowest levels to meet customer demands. Facebook was listed for its competitive culture and use of open workspaces to give employees an equal chance to succeed. There are many other examples, such as Progressive Insurance for promoting a culture of customer service. Procter & Gamble boasts a positive culture of employee collaboration. The "Chevron Way" is the motto of Chevron Corporation and establishes a common understanding for employees and customers of their cultural values, principles, and goals.

Organizational Culture also may be reflected in a number of operating practices, such as collaboration, innovation, flexibility, communication, employee expectations, philosophy, responsibility, management support and others. So, how do new leaders figure out what the corporate culture is when so many areas may be involved and, certainly, not all employees operate in the exact same way? They observe and actively listen to their followers and coworkers.

"Until I came to IBM, I probably would have told you that culture was just one among several important elements in any organization's makeup and success— along with vision, strategy, marketing, financials, and the like . . . I came to see, in my time at IBM, that culture isn't just one aspect of the game, it is the game. In the end, an organization is nothing more than the collective capacity of its people to create value."

—LOUIS V. GERSTNER
Former Chairman and CEO, IBM

ORGANIZATION AS A SYSTEM MODEL

A tool for analyzing an organization that encompasses a wide perspective and bridges across all the fuzzy lines of a bureaucracy is called the *Organization as a System* model and builds on a "Systems Thinking" method of analysis. Systems Thinking expands the analysis of a department, branch, or even a roadblock to discover where and how it interacts with other sectors of the company. Such a view may reveal touch points between organizational sectors that experience issues, overlaps, or redundancies.

Traditional analytical methods often drill down to the most minute of detail to identify a problem and its root causes. This more narrow and focused analytical technique dives deeply into the policies, practices and procedures of the department, branch or roadblock being reviewed or assessed.

For example, if a new leader wished to better understand her Human Resources department, she could consider two approaches: The traditional approach would have her spending time poring over HR records, reports, surveys, and staff and employee rosters. The Systems Thinking approach would find her identifying and assessing the type, frequency, and context for HR interaction with administration, technology or other company sectors. As part of this review, she may also look for key blockages, concerns and overlaps that HR has with other departments and, to deepen her analysis, learn the issues, concerns and touch points other organizational sectors had with HR.

Common questions (and often complaints) of new leaders when deciding to analyze their organizations are what to do, how to do it, and where to begin. What are you supposed to do first? When are you supposed to start? Can you do this yourself, or do you need permission?

The following model has proven to be helpful in orienting new leaders and managers to their institutions, as well as for rapidly identifying key problem areas and/or complaints experienced throughout the various sectors and hierarchical levels.

ORGANIZATION AS A SYSTEM

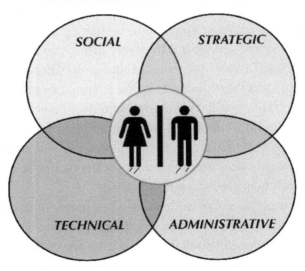

Exhibit 3: Organization as a System Model

This model partitions any organization into four sectors, each encompassing a number of people, resources, customers, finances, personal relationships, key documents, and interfaces.

SOCIAL: This sector generally includes human resources, client relationships, teams, employee relationships, key personnel, conflicts, training, employee morale, and reputation.

STRATEGIC: This sector typically includes vision statements, mission statements, strategic plans, partnerships, key corporate documents, goals, and business development.

TECHNICAL: This sector often includes technology, marketing, resources, employee skills, sales, equipment, distribution, and supply.

ADMINISTRATIVE: This sector may include legal, contracts, business processes, forms, manuals, budgets, policies, and bureaucracy.

SUMMARY

The use of this model sometimes confuses new leaders, since it views and analyzes their organizations from a big picture perspective. Larger institutions are especially complex, with multiple sectors, diverse clientele and numerous products and/or services.

The study of temperament also can be helpful when analyzing a company using the *Organization as a System* model. Although all four sectors boast personnel with all four dominant temperaments, the broad characterization of each temperament can provide guidance for planning an organizational analysis and questions that a new leader might ask.

Organization Sector	Dominant Temperament	Analysis Question
Social	Water	How do people in this sector succeed?
Strategic	Air	Does this sector "Walk the Talk" or rely on platitudes and dreams?
Technical	Fire	How often does this sector operate in "crisis mode" and how flexible is it in trying new technologies?
Administrative	Earth	How do sector requirements aid or inhibit the other sectors?

This analytical tool can help new leaders lead inquiries and information seeking efforts concerning various parts of the organization. It can be presented to followers and coworkers to illustrate the "big picture" and focus attention on where, when, and how these sectors intersect. Exploring this model even further requires the reader or course participant to select a sector then identify sub-sectors within it. For example, if the "Social" sector included HR, client relationships, team development and training (just to mention a few), each of them would be represented as a circle within the "Social" circle, and the analysis would include identifying the type, frequency and context for their intersections.

INFLUENCING ORGANIZATIONAL CHANGE

A John Maxwell quote in Chapter Two stated leadership is nothing more than influence—that is, leaders attempt to influence their followers into doing something they probably wouldn't do on their own.

On the face of it, there's nothing wrong with that description. If a leader tells her followers *this is the way to go* but has neither established trust nor credibility, then there really is no influence. Additionally, if she has not "walked the talk" nor possesses a great reputation, no one will follow her except those fearful of the negative consequences of her Position Power. Her vision would be nothing more than a wild dream that will never ever be realized. However, if she has developed trust and credibility and has a reputation for being of service to others and her organization, influence will indeed be present and followers will, well . . . follow.

Bestselling authors Teresa de Grosbois and Karen Rowe, in their masterful book "*Mass Influence: The Habits of the Highly Influential*," posit that there are 10 habits one should adopt to become skilled at influencing in an organization.

Habit #1: Playing Big

Influential people are of high service to others. Earlier it was pointed out that new leaders often find themselves hiding in their offices, poring over manuals, documents and plans, and rarely emerge to see what's actually happening in their organizations. How will you be of service to others when you don't interact with them? It's impossible. New leaders need to quickly identify the critical problems facing their institutions and the key people involved. Find out how the problems have been dealt with before (if they have) and begin to develop strategies for addressing them.

Influential people focus on the problem to the exclusion of all else. New leaders often overextend themselves. They take on too much too soon. Wanting to be helpful and of service to others can mean it's difficult to say no to requests for help. Dominant Water temperaments find this can be particularly frustrating and daunting since they value team approaches and the development of people no matter where they sit in the company's hierarchy.

Influential people know their fear is of no value to others. In order to be successful at *Playing Big*, new leaders must be self-confident in their skill, abilities and determination to solve problems that matter most to their organizations. Remember the Four Fatal Fears of Maxie Maultsby in Chapter One? Personal fear can paralyze progress and prevent taking necessary action. New leaders must resolve and steel themselves against letting fear get the better of them. A handy reminder for what fear stands for is: **F**alse **E**vidence **A**ppearing **R**eal (FEAR).

Habit #2: Authenticity

Influential people do something they really care about. Colvard has taught that having a stellar reputation is the best path to achieving real influence in an organization. That means earning the trust and respect of fellow employees enables and generates the development of influence. Being perceived by others as inauthentic—or playing a role or using a leadership position only as a stepping stone to some other line of work—will not result in building trust and respect. Demonstrating a deep commitment to the welfare of the organization is key to enhancing influence with coworkers, colleagues and other personnel. What drives your emotion and motivation for becoming a leader?

Influential people only play with others they deeply respect. Have you ever watched someone be charming in front of the boss but act just the opposite to everyone else when the boss leaves?

It's the "Eddie Haskell" effect (for those readers old enough to remember "*Leave It to Beaver!*") Those who do their work solely to gain points with their supervisors—and to the detriment of others—are not the people with whom new leaders want to spend their time. While trying to be helpful to all, new leaders will quickly identify those whom they can respect and trust. Those are the people most worthy of the time and effort it takes to establish a positive working relationship.

Habit #3: One-to-Many

Influential people spend much of their time communicating in a one-to-many scenario. While all members of an organization serve as their potential audience, new leaders often make the mistake of only developing personal working relationships with a single person or a small group. This reduces the impact of their communication in general and slows efforts to become more influential within an organization. Grab any opportunity to widen the scope of communication by speaking at committee meetings and brownbag lunch conferences. Contribute to in-house media, including newsletters and website columns or blogs.

Habit #4: Influence is a Currency

Influential people use influence as a currency of relationship building. A new leader will go out of his way to be friendly and welcoming to his followers, coworkers, colleagues, and executives as he takes over his new role and responsibilities. This friendliness should not be confused with influence.

Highly influential people will use their own growing influence to build relationships with other influential people in their organization. Methods may include: making introductions to key clients or networks of clients; accepting invitations to speak at conferences or other business gatherings; inclusion on technical panels; and, mentions in social media with a broad professional audience. Influencers are always on the lookout for win-win situations where their spheres of influence are widened through their participation in social events.

Habit #5: Building Powerful Relationships with Other Influencers

Influential people assertively seek out and build relationships with other influential people whom they respect and admire, regardless of the area in which they hold influence. When trying to introduce a change in an organization, new leaders are often bogged down by having to repeatedly argue their point of view with people who are resistant to the change. While resistance to change is normal and actually healthy for an organization (it can protect tradition and corporate reputation), time would be better spent moving on to those early adopters of the change—those who are immediately supportive and are influenced by the new leader.

Building relationships with supporters and other early adopters of an organizational change is more effective than continually fighting with naysayers. Even influencers in other disciplines can be helpful to the new leader in introducing change. For example, influencers in a technical or strategic discipline may support an administrative change, although their discipline may only interface with the change on occasion. Unlike a powerful administrative influencer who may deal with the change on a daily basis, influencers from other disciplines may provide key support to change efforts. Developing a strong relationship with them may be critical to the successful adoption of the change.

Habit #6: Understanding the Cycle of Reciprocity

Influential people build powerful relationships through powerful cycles of reciprocity. In the Marshall Islands, out in the Central Pacific, a cultural characteristic is reciprocity. If someone does something for you, you are expected to return the favor. On a small, narrow atoll with the ocean on one side and a lagoon on the other, this cultural norm reduces conflict for its tiny population and creates influencers. The most powerful influencers are those islanders who can do the most for others, no matter what people think of them personally. The internal drive to reciprocate, even if it's not at an equal level, is virtually overwhelming to the Marshallese. In organizations the basic rules of reciprocity also apply. Your feeling of obligation to reciprocate will outweigh your personal opinion of the giver. Whether you like someone or not, understanding their needs can lead to mutual respect and admiration over time.

Coined by author Shawne Duperon, this "cycle of reciprocity" is alive and well in the business world. New leaders who can build relationships with powerful influencers will strive to find opportunities to "return the favor" of influence—the currency of powerful influencers.

Habit #7: Connecting the Connectors

Influential people consistently connect the connectors. Often, within a single organization, the most powerful influencers will already know each other. Chances are, they'll have worked together or have been connected on a project or a task force or a committee. New leaders, especially those coming from a different branch or a division in a different location, may be able to connect key influencers to each other, or they may even be able to connect them with influencers from outside the organization, such as clients, media and competitors. Since influencers benefit from building powerful relationships with other influencers and from participating in a cycle of reciprocity, introducing influencers to each other is a great way to encourage collaboration.

Habit #8: Become a Hub for Other Influencers

Influential people serve their community by becoming a hub for other influencers. New leaders, over time, can boost their own credibility and influence by becoming a central "repository" of influence resources. This hub may be a learning community or a network within an organization where the new leader hosts a chat room or panel discussion with other influencers, even those from different technical disciplines. By virtue of taking the lead on developing a hub and being perceived by others in the company

123

as having the influence to establish such a high-level mastermind platform, the influence of the new leader grows.

Habit #9: Engaging and Enrolling Others

Influential people are masters at engaging and enrolling others. In Chapter Two, one of *The Five Practices of Exemplary Leadership* is "Inspiring a Shared Vision." This habit of influential people supports this leadership practice. The ability to paint a picture of a future organization and garner the support of followers is an important skill and successful practice of effective leaders.

Whether or not the opportunity immediately arises to identify a few influencers to share a vision and obtain their input, it's an effective strategy for new leaders to build a hub and grow it as fast as possible by engaging as large an audience as possible.

Habit #10: Influencers Take Action

Influential people routinely and repetitively take action toward achieving their goals and seek guidance when they don't know exactly what to do and how to do it. If new leaders read their books, attend their training courses, and make great plans for achieving widespread influence throughout their organizations but *NEVER TAKE ACTION,* nothing will ever happen. The highly influential leader takes action and, when faced with difficulties and conflicts, finds help to figure out the best way forward.

> *"Producing major change in an organization is not just about signing up one charismatic leader. You need a group—a team—to be able to drive the change. One person, even a terrific, charismatic leader, is never strong enough to make all this happen."*
>
> —JOHN P. KOTTER
> *Professor of Leadership, Emeritus, Harvard Business School*

ASKING EFFECTIVE QUESTIONS

In journalism school, students learn the five key questions every reporter needs to ask: Who, What, Where, When and Why. There's also a How. This allows reporters to rapidly get to the heart of a situation and kick-starts the development of a story when they're working under pressure of a deadline.

Although asking "Why" can take time and is more often in the purview of the novelist or author, it's important to find out why things happen. Leaders, especially new leaders, typically don't have a lot of time and often must make decisions with little or no information.

Asking open-ended questions (such as "How did you. . . ?"; "How will you. . . ?"; "How can you. . . ?"; and "What will you. . . ?") allows responders to tell their stories while leaders listen to gain understanding. Pausing to reflect on the following categories of questions allows one time to be intentional rather than reactive in responding. Taking this extra time can significantly enhance the quality of leadership interactions.

Here's a brief summary of the basic categories of questions with some examples that may be helpful to new leaders and managers. You can use these types of questions to direct organizational teams and groups toward achieving tasks and goals (see Four Energetic Directions of Questions in Chapter Three).

QUESTIONS THAT CLARIFY AND PROBE
- Who is the source of this information?
- What are the greatest information gaps?
- When will we need to complete our analysis?
- Where can we discover additional information?
- Why are we working on this particular issue?
- How can we obtain additional information?

QUESTIONS THAT IDENTIFY IMPACT AND CONSEQUENCES

- Who will be negatively impacted by the solution?
- What are the potential negative repercussions?
- When is it most effective to implement our strategy?
- Where in the organization should we be most concerned?
- Why will the department's reputation be at risk?
- How can we address resistance to change?

QUESTIONS THAT ENGAGE OTHERS IN PROBLEM-SOLVING

- Who are the best people we can find?
- What are the team's best ideas?
- When is the issue reaching a critical state?
- Where should we begin?
- Why should other employees join our team?
- How can we make it better?

QUESTIONS THAT EMPOWER

- Who can we engage to manage this approach?
- What would be a better way to strategize?
- When do you want to start?
- Where do we find the resources needed to solve this problem?
- Why is it important to get executive buy-in?
- How can we effectively get this task done?

While these categories and questions can be helpful and important to new leaders, there may also be a downside to efforts to ask effective questions that can be detrimental and dysfunctional:

DISEMPOWERING QUESTIONS

- Who do you think you are?
- What was going through your mind when you did that?
- When were you going to tell the rest of us?
- Where on earth are you going with this line of thinking?

- Why would you do that?
- How will you ever recover from that?

Remember that children's game called "Telephone"? A number of kids would arrange themselves in a large circle. The first child would whisper something into the ear of the second child, who would pass it along to the next child, and so forth. The last child to hear the message tells the group what she heard, and it's always different, and funnier, than the initial message. This game shows an important distinction between hearing and listening. Many texts will tell you *hearing* is more of a biological function based on the physicality of the ear. *Listening*, however, is more of a linguistic function and involves actively focusing on the speaker and interpretation of the message's meaning.

An effective exercise on the subject requires pairs of participants to sit knee-to-knee after agreeing to discuss a controversial issue where each holds opposing views. The speaker has two minutes to share her perspective and position while the listener must remain silent. After two minutes, the speaker remains silent for a minute while the listener summarizes what he heard the speaker say. This is not a word-for-word recitation of what was heard but rather a meaningful understanding of the first speaker's position. After the minute expires, the first speaker has an additional uninterrupted minute to agree, disagree or clarify what the listener just said. After that minute, the listener has one more uninterrupted minute to re-state the last clarification, whereas the first speaker then agrees or disagrees that the listener has indeed understood her communication. Then positions are reversed, the listener becomes the speaker, and the exercise continues until there is mutual understanding.

> *"Most people do not listen with the intent to understand; they listen with the intent to reply."*
>
> —Stephen Covey
> *Author of "The 7 Habits of Highly Effective People"*

THE FOUR ENERGETIC DIRECTIONS OF QUESTIONS

Leaders need to listen to the responses to their questions. When asked to name the characteristics of an ideal leader, NASA and U.S. Navy leadership training participants list "Listening" among their top answers.

Effective leaders often find themselves wanting to steer follower groups in the direction of developing better strategies and understanding for solving conflicts and problems. Any group may be led in four *directions*, yet each direction will call upon group members to take into consideration their personal and organizational values, their individual temperament, their foundational personalities and their intuition.

Quick Leadership Group (QLG) instructor Jim White has developed a model for helping leaders facilitate team or group discussions through the use of questions. *The Four Energetic Directions of Questions* is based on the concept that energy in the organization can be generated and focused based on the type of questions asked by the facilitator, team leader or another group member. These directions include:

> **PURPOSE:** Questions a leader can ask in this direction encourages groups (or individuals) within the group or team to look beyond the specifics of what has been or should have been tried before; what has or hasn't worked; or, what has completely failed. The focus here is on the higher meaning, the "for the sake of what," and the intention of the issue rather than playing the "blame game." For example, if a follower group is focused on increasing future sales, a leader might ask, "What's the higher purpose of our debating new sales techniques? Is it to generate more revenue? Is it to

achieve goals we promised our shareholders? Is it to ensure our sales force operates more effectively as a team?" Or, "For the sake of what are we considering changing the way we conduct our sales approach and strategy?"

PRESENT: Questions a leader can ask in this direction lead the group toward expressing their current feelings about the issue or topic. The focus is on generating energy to explore the immediate mood and/or reactions to what is happening and not dwelling on past failures or disappointments. For example, the leader might ask, "How does everyone feel about it now? What are your current thoughts on what we might do to solve the situation?" Or, "What organizational values are you most concerned about losing in our situation?"

PAST: Questions a leader can ask in this direction often lead the group back toward a rehashing of past mistakes in an attempt to solve the current problem. Focusing the group on the past can remind and inform them of specific approaches, methods and attempts that were tried. However, recollections from the past do not tell the group what's needed to solve a current or future situation and often generate negative energy. It's nearly impossible to dwell in the past and try to imagine the future at the same time. For example, the leader may ask, "What are the root causes of this situation? What occurred in the past that led us to where we are today?" Or, "What bothers you most about how this situation was dealt with by the previous administration?"

FUTURE: Questions in this direction enable a leader to pull a team or group towards the future by focusing on what's possible or imaginable. This direction is characterized by divergent thinking to generate energy around discovering themes and patterns that can lead to transformational approaches. This is where techniques like brainstorming or mind mapping are helpful. For example, the leader may ask, "How do you envision this situation turning out? What can you expect in the future?" Or, "How will we address the issue of amending required skill sets for our workforce going forward?"

Neuroscience tells us different parts of the neural networks in our brains are used when focusing on the past, present or future. Jim White's "*The 4 Energetic Directions of Questions*," taken from his longer article entitled "The Art, Craft and Science of Facilitating Transformational Workshops," informs new leaders that their goal is to move groups and teams toward new possibilities rather than dwelling on past failures. A major dissection and analysis of what was done right and what was done wrong won't necessarily lead to a successful future solution. In fact, that approach often results in a downward spiral of team negativity, second-guessing and a lowering of morale. For this reason, White recommends leaders should ask questions that direct their followers to the future.

SUMMARY

The purpose of asking questions is not only to obtain direct answers and better understand the speaker's opinions. It's also to generate group energy in a direction or line of thinking the leader wants her group to take. Leaders can direct the attention of organizational groups and focus them on exploring, analyzing and even brainstorming concerns, roadblocks and problems to identify the best solutions possible. The effective leader is one who realizes she does not hold all the answers and recognizes a responsibility for asking the crucial questions needed to lead her team toward achieving team goals and objectives.

"Successful people ask better questions, and as a result, they get better answers."

—TONY ROBBINS
American Author & Motivational Speaker

THE 4 ENERGETIC DIRECTIONS OF QUESTIONS

From "The Art, Craft and Science of Facilitating Transformational Workshops."

By Jim White

Exhibit 4: The 4 Energetic Directions of Questions

At the end of the third week of instruction, the course partici-pant will connect again with the Strategic Leadership Advisor (SLA) by phone or online. It is anticipated he/she will have a number of questions about leading in an organization. On-the-job experiences and knowledge gained through live instruction will also inform their discussions. Readers will find SLA questions useful for self-instruction and debriefings with a coach or mentor.

- How would you describe your organization? Describe its bureaucracy. How does it operate?

- What did you learn about your organization by analyzing it using the *Organization as a System* model?

- What is keeping your organization from being run optimally?

- What will be expected of you as a new leader when it comes to reviewing, writing and submitting reports?

- What is the process for employee performance reviews? Will you be responsible for them? What has been your experience in conducting them?

- How might your corporate culture prevent you from becoming an effective leader? How might it help?

- How confident are you that you will be able to influence your organization?

- If you had an idea that changed how a process was implemented, how would you proceed in making that change a reality?

- How have you used *Emotional Intelligence* this week?

- What document would you rely on most to provide a "big picture" view of your organization's financial health?

- What are some ways to build trust in your organization?

- What lessons did you learn from the leadership instruction you received this week?

- What did you learn about yourself as a leader this week?

The following are sample assignments participants and readers may complete by the end of their third program week. The successes or remaining tasks of each assignment are discussed at the end of the week with the Strategic Leadership Advisor, coach or mentor.

Sample Assignments:

1. Analyze your organization using the *Organization as a System* model. Identify the areas where you have a strong influencing network and areas of little or no influence.

2. Describe your corporate culture.

3. Spend time with the financial officials of your organization. What are the financial documents or reports that leaders are provided on a routine basis?

4. Review the basic documents of your organization (such as mission statement, vision statement, strategic plan.)

5. Identify the various types of reports you will be expected to review, write and submit as a new leader.

6. What are the greatest impediments facing your organization over the next three years? The next five years?

7. Research a recent organizational change. How was it introduced? What were the issues? Was there resistance? How was it handled?

8. Identify your major customers, clients and stakeholders.

9. Use *Emotional Intelligence* to handle a conflict within your organization.

10. Describe your organization's vision in under five minutes.

11. Review this week's leadership instruction. What made the greatest impact on you? How might you apply what you learned on the job?

12. Be ready to discuss how you rate your progress in becoming an effective leader.

The following is a sample checklist participants may be asked to complete by their third program week. Checklists are designed to remind participants of work that needs to be done during the week and provides a method for keeping track of their progress. The checklist may be reviewed and discussed at the end of the week with the Strategic Leadership Advisor. Readers may find the checklist useful for self-improvement.

Sample Checklist Items:

1. Identify organizational areas of influence. ☐
2. Identify corporate culture. ☐
3. Identify key financial documents. ☐
4. Review basic organizational documents. ☐
5. Identify reports I'll need to review, write and submit. ☐
6. Identify critical organizational concerns over next 3-5 years. ☐
7. Research a recent organizational change. ☐
8. Identify major customers, clients and stakeholders. ☐
9. Use EI to handle a conflict. ☐
10. Articulate my organization's vision statement in 5 minutes. ☐
11. Identify most important lessons learned this week. ☐
12. Rate my leadership progress this week on a scale of 1 to 10. ☐

CHAPTER FOUR

WEEK 3:
(OPTIONAL)
PRACTICUM

The new "Quick! I Need to Be a Leader in 30 Days!" course offers an optional practicum for organizations wishing to enroll eight or more participants at once. This group size allows for the logistical arrangements of a two-day, off-site session using experiential technologies to learn about leading organizations while building self-confidence and team spirit.

Creating change and fostering growth requires participant engagement physically, emotionally and intellectually. In any training program that offers an experiential component, participants have the opportunity to determine levels of involvement appropriate for them. Whatever experiential methodology used—theater, service projects, ropes courses or adventure activities—instruction is designed to support the overall transformational effort in the participants' organization and should not be considered ends in themselves.

One of the key models offered during this optional session is the decision-making approach called The Results-Model (also offered during Week 3: Leading Organizations.)

THE RESULTS-MODEL

Developed by QLG instructor Jeff Whitehead and others, this model aids the new leader or manager in examining personal decision-making methods and clarifying thought processes.

It all starts with an *event*. Something happens that comes to your awareness. Whitehead uses business theorist and educator Chris Argyris's "Ladder of Inference" to demonstrate a mental model illustrating how one's personal beliefs can lead to an incorrect interpretation of an event no matter the data or behaviors one observes. By means of illustration, Whitehead selects a workshop participant and whispers for her to say hello to him as she walks by, as if in a common hallway. They repeat the scenario with other participants watching closely as she says hello while Whitehead says nothing in reply and refuses to even make eye contact.

The volunteer returns to the large group of her fellow participants as Whitehead asks them to call out some adjectives describing his behavior. "Jerk," is one of the nicer words he hears back from the group. He pushes them to systematically examine their thought process, and it's revealed they've added meaning to his action (taking the first step up the Ladder of Inference). They believe he's being insulting and insensitive, since the norm is to respond in kind to someone who greets you (taking yet another step up the ladder.) They assume he lives in his own elitist world and cares nothing about the feelings of others (another rung up the ladder.) They conclude he probably acts that way to everybody, and agree they'd never want to work with someone like that and would avoid him in the future (finally reaching the top of the Ladder of Inference.)

Whitehead points out that climbing up all rungs of the Ladder of Inference (i.e., experience, selection of data, meanings, assumptions, conclusions and future actions) happens rapidly in one's mind yet can be totally *misguided*. He finishes the demonstration by asking if their rapid journey of jumping to conclusions would be different if they knew his character in the scenario had just heard his small daughter was hurt in a car accident, and he couldn't get through to the hospital on the phone to check on her.

The various steps in the Ladder of Inference are based on a *Mental Map* everyone carries around in their heads. It's created by experiences, temperament, beliefs, values, culture, education and other factors. Referring back to the previous demonstration, Whitehead asks, "What's your Mental Map for saying hello in a hallway?" Personal experience, organizational culture and values tell group members to immediately respond with a friendly greeting while making eye contact. The group's negative descriptive labels, however, illustrated that when an event, behavior or experience violated their Mental Maps, they *made stuff up* about Whitehead's character and acted as if all of their negative labels were true.

Whitehead goes on to ask the group if they would prefer to drive from Washington D.C. to Miami using a map from 1956 or one from today. He points out that it's critical to ensure a leader's Mental Map is current and constantly being updated. How are they updated? By taking a deep breath and pausing before scrambling up the Ladder of Inference; and, challenging your assumptions.

The Results-Model acknowledges that everyone responds differently to the events around them. Individuals respond internally by feeling mad, sad, glad or scared about an event and/or respond externally through personal behavior. When a leader is feeling less than positive or neutral about a response to an experience, they should stop! Take a breath! Check on the last update of their

Mental Map as determined by their reaction. Check to see if they are *making stuff up* about the event. Effective external responses should more likely lead to desired long-term results rather than short-term comfort.

In Whitehead's earlier demonstration, the immediate feelings that emerged from the group were negative (Why didn't he say hello or look at her?). Instead they should have taken a deep breath and considered the Mental Map they were using (Gee, he acted strangely). Next they should have wondered what was going on with him and pondered what they may have been *making up* about that scenario (Is he just a jerk, or is something wrong?). The response to be taken is the next consideration. (Should we stay away from that guy, or stop by to ask what's going on with him?) Finally, they should have evaluated which response would have helped them achieve a long-term desired result.

SUMMARY

Decision-making is obviously a critical skill for any new leader. If promotions to a new leadership position are based primarily on technical expertise, it's probably a reflection of the candidate making technically correct and organizationally effective decisions. As a leader, your spheres of influence widen rapidly, and there will be personal involvement with many more concerns than the routine technical obstructions that once ruled the day and led to your enhanced reputations and increased responsibilities.

The Results-Model asks leaders to analyze observations, interpretations of events and knee-jerk reactions to the behaviors they experience. It asks them to make decisions that have long-term results that positively influence events in their organizations. It asks leaders to reflect upon their personal biases and prejudices before making decisions that could damage reputations and turn small misunderstandings into major conflicts.

THE RESULTS-MODEL

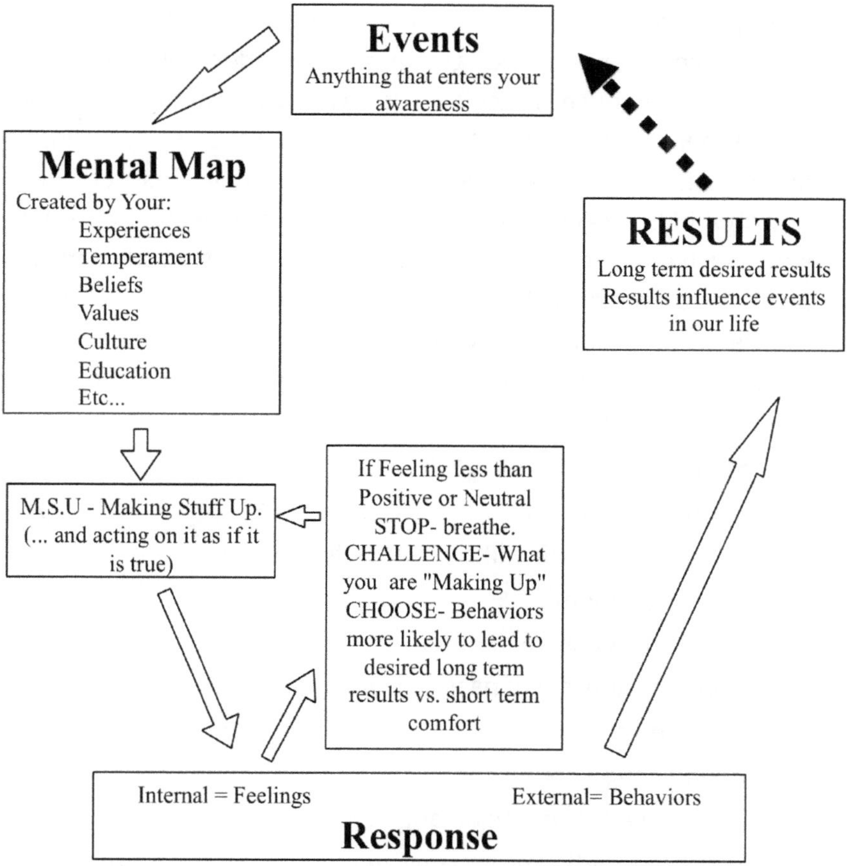

Events
Anything that enters your awareness

Mental Map
Created by Your:
    Experiences
    Temperament
    Beliefs
    Values
    Culture
    Education
    Etc...

RESULTS
Long term desired results
Results influence events in our life

M.S.U - Making Stuff Up. (... and acting on it as if it is true)

If Feeling less than Positive or Neutral STOP- breathe. CHALLENGE- What you are "Making Up" CHOOSE- Behaviors more likely to lead to desired long term results vs. short term comfort

Internal = Feelings   External= Behaviors

Response

Exhibit 5: The Results-Model

BUILDING SELF-CONFIDENCE

"One important key to success is self-confidence. An important key to self-confidence is preparation."

—ARTHUR ASHE
World No. 1 Tennis Star

In preparing yourself to be an effective leader can't you feel your self-confidence already growing? New leaders will, of course, experience nervousness and even get a bit scared at times as they learn the ins and outs of their new jobs. However, such feelings are actually forms of fear (see Four Fatal Fears in Chapter One) and should be acknowledged as normal and expected. It's only when such emotions paralyze leadership actions that steps must be taken to overcome these troublesome emotions.

There are a number of books and articles on how leaders can become more self-confident. Some of the methods and techniques you may read about include:

- Setting and achieving goals
- Studying the brain
- Acting and dressing like a successful person
- Self-assessment
- Acting in a positive manner
- Keeping a journal of past achievements
- Meditating
- Taking action
- Being assertive in use of language

In order to rapidly prepare new leaders to "hit the ground running" in their new positions, a few of these confidence-building techniques will now be addressed and a few more in later chapters.

Self-assessment is critical to the success of any new leader and the reader should, by now, have identified a dominant, secondary, tertiary and shadow temperament to provide insight into personal preferences and a view of the world. Readers also should have completed Personal Skill Challenges and Personal Development Challenges inventories to identify specific areas they want to work on and build upon in the world of leadership.

At the end of each chapter (and end of each week of live course instruction), it is suggested that readers (and participants) keep a personal *journal* of reactions, questions, and their successes and remaining concerns to on-the-job experiences as they apply new leadership models, concepts and practices.

Taking action is another weekly task for readers and course participants. A more formal Action Plan (see Chapter Five) encourages readers to compile and plan specific leadership development actions in a three-, six- and 12-month time frame.

Studying the brain is another useful preparation area for new leaders. An understanding of how the human brain is hardwired to have negative biases comes from Dr. Rick Hanson's book, *"Buddha's Brain."* Hanson tells us, "The bad is like Velcro; the good is like Teflon and to change the Velcro to Teflon we need to take in and hold the good in our awareness (for at least 20 seconds)."

Negative "self-talk" happens to everybody. That little voice inside our heads may tell us horrible things like we can't make it as a leader; we're not smart enough; we're not clever enough; and we're just fooling everyone. That voice urges new leaders to look for the negative in their work life and to continually find fault with followers and coworkers while nitpicking things they don't like about their organizations. This self-talk or inner narrative, much like the fear of failure, can make new leaders and managers avoid taking risks and extending themselves to help others. It also can raise anxiety levels and cause debilitating stress.

So, how can this negative self-talk be avoided? Unfortunately, it can't. However, its impact can be diminished, as Hanson suggests, by making a special effort to find the positives in our work life and celebrating what's right rather than always looking for what's wrong.

Human brains have an immense capacity to learn. Over time, they can change themselves in small ways based on the blood flow and oxygen they receive, particularly from emotional experiences that affect biological processes. This capacity is called *neuroplasticity* and, according to Hanson, involves the changing of the brain's "physical tissues, which affect your well-being, functioning, and relationships."

Hanson informs readers that making positive experiences more prominent than negative experiences in our minds will gradually reduce the impact of negative self-talk. This gradual balancing relationship between positive and negative experiences is similar to the exploration of hidden talents within the shadow temperament (see Chapter One). While the negative aspects of shadow behaviors are easily perceived and often deeply felt, over time, a better understanding of their more positive aspects (such as undiscovered skills and interests), can restore a balance and enhance their more positive characteristics.

Larger groups of participants enrolled in the "Quick! I Need to Be a Leader in 30 Days!" live course may opt for two days of experiential learning during their third week of instruction. The physical and mental stimulation of high rope climbing, team puzzle solving, pole scaling and other interactive exercises focus not on overcoming personal fears, but rather on individual growth as a fundamental element within a team or organization to promote healthy, effective company cultures. QLG instructor Jeff Whitehead said, "It's not really about conquering fear, but finding courage and working *through* fear."

"The secret of making dreams come true can be summa-
rized in four Cs. They are Curiosity, Confidence, Courage,
and Constancy; and the greatest of these is Confidence."

—WALT DISNEY
Entrepreneur

For many new leaders, building self-confidence is a dream that requires hard work and diligent preparation.

BUILDING TRUST

One of the most important skills a new leader must develop is the ability to generate trust among followers, coworkers, colleagues and executive management. It's also one of the easiest skills to mess up. Without trust, one may hold the *title* of leader or manager, but who will follow except those who are frightened of the negative consequences for disobeying? A leader without any real followers is not really a leader.

So, what does it take to build trust and keep that trust viable throughout a leadership career? Here are 25 guidelines and practices that a number of leaders in the field of business, government and the non-profit sector have proven to be successful.

HOW TO BUILD TRUST

- Do be truthful. Leaders who tell one-person one thing and another person something else are bound to trip up, and will certainly lose the trust of both.
- Do be consistent. Maintaining a uniform approach to work and to the workforce will enable followers to view you as dependable.
- Do communicate daily with the workforce. Ensure that followers have access to you when needed.
- Do make promises and keep them. Demonstrate you are a person of your word and a leader to be counted on to do what you say you'll do.
- Do set an example. *Modeling the Way* can set a high bar for organizational excellence and demonstrates strong commitment.
- Don't always believe what you see.
- Do be a good listener. Listen to understand the needs of the workforce.
- Do keep confidential conversations in confidence. Credibility increases when followers understand that leaders can keep secrets.
- Don't over-promise. Leaders get in trouble when they believe they can "save" their followers, teams, and departments.
- Do play an active role in your organization. The more leaders involve themselves in the daily routines of their organizations, the more they're able to be influencers.
- Do trust yourself to do the right thing.
- Do let your followers know that you trust them.
- Do be optimistic. Believing something is possible will help make it so. A positive attitude increases follower appreciation and respect.

- Do be collaborative. Look for opportunities to work with followers on task forces, teams and committees.
- Do trust others. Some leaders believe trust must be earned while others believe it should be given. Neither is wrong.
- Do be responsible. Accept responsibilities for your actions and for those who report to you.
- Don't share gossip. A very quick way to ruin trust is when accusations arise based on gossip you've created or shared.
- Do be honest. Effective leaders admit when they're wrong or do not know.
- Do share your thoughts and feelings. Let followers know what's in your heart and mind, and they will eventually do the same with you.
- Do serve as a mentor or coach. Assist followers, coworkers and/or colleagues by establishing formal mentor or coaching relationships.
- Don't be afraid of making mistakes. Everyone expects their leaders to make mistakes. It's what leaders do with those mistakes that matters most.
- Don't over think the process of building trust. Do the right thing; having good intentions and making a positive effort will be enough.
- Do realize earning the trust of others takes time. This effort is built on one-to-one transactions over time.
- Do not lie but recognize that sometimes you will be prevented from telling the whole truth.
- Don't always take the popular position. Do what's right.

"Trust is the essence of leadership."

—COLIN POWELL
Former General, U.S. Army

According to authors Kouzes and Posner, a 2009 international study found that most people trusted a stranger more than they trusted their boss! Trust has to do with personal credibility, organizational performance and the willingness of employees to be influenced. Trust is another critical element of being a successful leader, and it starts with the leader trusting his followers!

The willingness to trust someone is linked to one's temperament. For example, engineers, scientists and administrators from NASA, the U.S. Navy, and other research centers, while undergoing a temperament session as a part of a leadership course, were divided into dominant temperament groups and reported on their willingness to trust a new employee:

TEMPERAMENT	WILLINGNESS TO TRUST
EARTH	New employees must earn their trust by doing good work over time, meeting deadlines and keeping their promises.
AIR	New employees with stellar reputations and credentials are immediately trusted; other new employees generally must earn their trust by demonstrating personal competence over time.
FIRE	New employees are immediately trusted until they prove to be inflexible, passive or lack a sense of humor.
WATER	New employees are immediately trusted until they prove to be liars, cheaters or steal from the organization.

For followers to trust a leader, it's incumbent upon the leader to take the first step. He needs to develop a working environment that followers believe is safe, fosters clear communication and is harmonious. Effective leaders take risks. They identify opportunities for followers to add value to the organization. This sometimes involves risk, and the leader must trust followers enough to let them fail—which may result in the leader suffering the consequences.

The effective leader who brings people together, cares about their visions, hopes and concerns, willingly takes risks, keeps promises and confidences and develops trusting relationships will gain the trust of their followers. In Chapter One, authors Colvard and Maxwell agreed that the highest form of power is the Power of Positive Reputation. It's earned by doing a job effectively and efficiently, by developing others, by becoming a role model, and by walking the talk—doing what you say you'll do—over time. It's how you gain the trust of others.

At end of the third optional week of instruction, participants will reconnect with their Strategic Leadership Advisor (SLA) by phone or online. This session will focus on the various experiential activities undergone earlier in the week and includes such leadership topics as building trust, developing self-confidence and team building. Readers may find the following discussion questions helpful for self-improvement.

- How would you describe your current level of confidence for becoming a new leader?

- How might you apply lessons learned from your experiential instruction this week?

- What was your approach to analyzing your organization using the *Organization as a System* model?

- How will you update your Mind Maps?

- How can you build the self-confidence of your followers? What methods might you use?

- What concerns or resistances do you anticipate when introducing a change in your organization? What will your first steps be to address the resistance?

- Do you trust your employees right from the start, or must they earn your trust? Describe your reasoning.

- What is keeping your organization from running efficiently and effectively? What steps would you take during the first six months in your new leadership position to make your team, division, department and/or organization operate optimally?

- What have you learned about the relationship between team-work, self-confidence and trust?

- How will you manage your workday?

- What lessons did you learn from the leadership instruction you received this week?

- What did you learn about yourself as a leader this week?

The following are sample assignments participants will complete by the end of the optional third week of our program. The successes or remaining tasks within each assignment are discussed at the end of the week with the Strategic Leadership Advisor. Readers may find these assignments helpful for self-improvement.

Sample Assignments:

1. Volunteer to lead a team on an organizational task.

2. Analyze your organization using the *Organization as a System* model. Identify areas where you have a strong influencing network and areas of little or no influence.

3. Jot down 5-10 bullet points describing your corporate culture.

4. Identify the 3-5 key financial documents that leaders are provided on a routine basis.

5. Identify the basic organizational documents of your company (such as mission statement, vision statement, strategic plan). Where are they physically located? Do all employees have access to them?

6. Identify the various types of reports you will be expected to review, write and submit as a new leader.

7. What Mental Maps are present in your organization?

8. Analyze your experiential activities this week and identify the ones that most increased your self-confidence.

9. Identify your major customers, clients and stakeholders.

10. How will you create a powerful coalition to lead change efforts?

11. Review this week's leadership instruction. What made the greatest impact on you? How might you apply what you learned on the job?

12. Be ready to discuss how you rate your progress in becoming an effective leader.

The following is a sample checklist participants may be asked to complete by the end of their optional third program week. Checklists are designed to remind participants of work that needs to be done during the week and provides a method for keeping track of their progress. The checklist may be reviewed and discussed at the end of the week with the Strategic Leadership Advisor. Readers may find the checklist useful for self-improvement.

Sample Checklist Items:

1. Describe my organization's corporate culture. ☐

2. Identify key financial documents. ☐

3. Review basic organizational documents. ☐

4. Identify reports to review, write, and submit. ☐

5. Identify organizational Mental Maps. ☐

6. Research a recent organizational change. ☐

7. Identify major customers, clients and stakeholders. ☐

8. Identify key experiential activities resulting in enhanced self-confidence. ☐

9. Identify most important lessons learned this week. ☐

10. Rate my leadership progress this week on a scale of 1 to 10. ☐

CHAPTER FIVE

WEEK 4:
LEADING INTO THE FUTURE

During the fourth and final week of the "Quick! I Need to Be a Leader in 30 Days!" certificate course, participants and readers will put together everything they've learned during the first three weeks as they gaze into their future roles as leaders. The development of an Action Plan for continuing your leadership development over the next three, six and 12 months is a course requirement and will be the focus of a live instructional module as well as a topic of discussion with the Strategic Leadership Advisor who'll provide suggestions and recommendations. This week will include the following topics:

Envisioning a Leadership Future
Role of the Strategic Leadership Advisor
Action Planning
Site Visit by Strategic Leadership Advisor
  – Leadership Practice Session with Feedback
  – Confidential Follower Feedback Session
  – Personal Feedback and Action Plan Review
  – Completion of Certification Process
  – Recommendations for Continuous Learning

ENVISIONING A LEADERSHIP FUTURE

The last full week of the program dares participants and readers to peer into their crystal balls and imagine what success in leadership looks like in the not too distant future. Now equipped with a number of practical models, tools and concepts, the burden on readers and participants is to make some sense of all their knowledge and experiences and apply them in the real world. Recall the metaphor of a "leadership toolbox" from which new leaders can select the appropriate concept, tool, or model they deem useful for the situation at hand.

QLG instructor Jim White has developed an amazing process for capturing the imagination of new leaders that assists them in focusing one year into a successful future and guiding them back in time to identify the key tasks and activities they implemented to achieve that future success. New leaders will imagine the workshops they attended or led; the feedback they received; the influencing networks they created; the followers whose skills they developed; the opportunities they found for their employees; the risks they took; the conflicts they managed; and the successes they celebrated.

This "envisioning" process will be guided by a QLG instructor in a live session and will aid the participant in prioritizing the key activities needed to be successful in his/her own organization. The results of this exercise also may inform parts of the required Action Plan and serve as another analytical tool for leadership planning.

The main idea is for readers and participants to predict the situations they anticipate in their new roles and mentally apply the leadership principles they believe will positively impact the people in their organization.

ROLE OF THE STRATEGIC LEADERSHIP ADVISOR

Although this important QLG faculty member will provide individual guidance and assistance to participants throughout the course, this role is especially significant during the Site Visit scheduled for Day 30. The Strategic Leadership Advisor (SLA) will be responsible for these tasks:

- Lead weekly participant debriefing sessions
- Facilitate a discussion on the impact of each week's live instruction
- Answer participant leadership questions
- Review participant checklists
- Review and discuss the week's on-the-job assignments
- Discuss the week's reading assignment
- Serve as a sounding board for participant on-the-job leadership experiences
- Clarify, as needed, assignments and readings for the week ahead
- Conduct a one-day visit to the participant's worksite during Day 30 to complete the following tasks:
  - Lead a confidential debriefing session with participant followers
  - Conduct a feedback session regarding certification requirements
  - Review Action Plans and provide suggestions and recommendations
  - Review the Impact Paper
  - Recommend continuous leadership learning instruction for the future
  - Approve or disapprove QLG Professional Leadership Certification

SITE VISIT BY THE STRATEGIC LEADERSHIP ADVISOR

Based on weekly conversations between the Strategic Leadership Advisor (SLA) and the participant throughout the course, a one-day site visit will be conducted to finalize the certification process, provide confidential feedback and make recommendations for continued leadership instruction. The SLA site visit will include the following:

Leadership Practice Session with Feedback

Participants are asked during the third week of the course to complete logistical arrangements for the SLA to observe an actual leadership activity (such as leading a meeting, making an announcement, conducting a mentoring or coaching session.) This activity, perhaps an hour or more in length, enables the SLA to get a feel for how the participant: interacts with followers; demonstrates effective leadership strategies; asks effective questions; shows personal openness; and, confirms a commitment to integrity.

Confidential Follower Feedback Session

Participants are also asked to arrange for the SLA to facilitate a confidential feedback session with a representative sample of followers. This session provides the SLA with an opportunity to gather specific feedback on the leadership performance of the participant during the past month. The SLA will search for eyewitness evidence that the participant actually practices the QLG certification requirement criteria in real time. Topics and questions by the SLA to the follower group may include:

- Describe a time when the participant demonstrated a commitment to organizational effectiveness.

- How would you describe the participant's understanding of leadership?
- What can you say about the participant's integrity?
- Describe how the participant provides support to you when you have been delegated a task.
- How open to your suggestions and recommendations is the participant?
- What would you say is the participant's leadership style?
- On a scale of 1 to 10 (10 being best) rate the timeliness of the participant in meeting deadlines, completing work and showing up for meetings with you.
- Can you provide an example of a time when the participant demonstrated a commitment to continuous improvement?
- What specific areas should the participant work on to become a more effective leader?

Action Planning

Participants and readers must balance their financial investments, time commitments and the specific leadership requirements they wish to study against the multitude of leadership courses they may wish to attend. However, courses that do not link leadership content to real-world concerns, conflicts and the Gordian Knots of problems new leaders face are not the best match. The course, "Quick! I Need to Be a Leader in 30 Days!" requires each participant to develop an Action Plan designed to shift his/her thinking from leadership theory to actual practice. Focusing on the first three, six and twelve months of on-the-job leadership implementation, the plan will be reviewed by the SLA during the site visit (if not before).

Action Planning is intended to generate a commitment to carry out specific tasks during your initial year after assuming a leadership position. Without a purpose, there can be no real commitment. New leaders must understand why they are making a plan and how it serves them and their organizations. Otherwise, Action Planning becomes just busy work.

There are templates available online to aid in the Action Planning process. Here is a suggested approach:

ACTION PLANNING: PREPARATION AND DESIGN

1. ACTION STEP: Written as a behavior or specific practice, list the steps that need to be taken to achieve the overall goal. There should be a separate Action Plan for a three-, six- and twelve-month period.

2. TIMELINE: For each Action Step, develop a timeline for completing it. Time periods may include ranges (such as four to six weeks) as well as specific dates.

3. WHO: The reader or participant will be the "who" in most Action Steps, however there may be other individuals that can be identified as the responsible party. For example, if an Action Step is to lead a team, the supervisor in charge of managing teams may be identified in the "Who" column.

4. RESOURCES NEEDED: Often new leaders have not given enough thought to what resources they need, nor what resources are available to them. This column may include books, online courses, master classes and/or coaching or mentoring.

5. EXPECTED RESULTS: New leaders may expect the results of their efforts will be the same as their Action Step. This may or may not be true. For example, if the Action Step is to lead a team/obtain approval and you're asked not to lead a team but rather *join* a team, the expected results would differ from your Action Step.

6. POSSIBLE ROADBLOCKS: This column is usually easiest to complete since roadblocks are prevalent in any organization.

The effective leader will not let possible roadblocks detour progress in achieving the Action Step.

7. EVALUATION: Particularly at the three-, six- and twelve-month points, it is important to assess progress in achieving goals and Action Steps. At the end of three months, anticipate that your goal and Action Steps may need revising to address the realities of the organization.

ACTION PLANNING GRID

Person Responsible

Goal: Implement Leadership Strategies Over the Next Year

Action Step	Timeline	Who	Resources Needed	Expected Results	Possible Roadblocks	Evaluation

ACTION PLANNING: WATCH OUT FOR THIS!

The expectation is for new leaders to be ready to lead by Day One. "After all," one might say, "didn't she just get the promotion to this position? She should know what she's doing." The process of action planning can be logical, organized and helpful to the new leader who is attempting to make sense out of a vague job description no one has time to clarify or explain in detail.

Typically, leadership duties are "add-ons" to other more technically focused duties and responsibilities. Developing an Action Plan is a positive and effective way to ensure leadership tasks do not get left behind in the push to "get the job done." However, action planners should be aware of the following pitfalls that can turn the planning process into a nightmare.

- *Not including key people.* New leaders need all the help they can get. Whether it's a coach, mentor or peer, be sure to include those who can provide insight and a sanity check for your plan. If you do receive input, be sure to show those folks how their input is reflected in your plan.

- *Planning too early in your new position.* Everyone wants to ensure they can assume their new roles and responsibilities rapidly and with minimal guidance. Take some time to explore the organization. Who are the key players? What are the available resources? What are the immediate topics of concern? Although there are continuous learning goals and action steps that may be identified from your readings or course, don't rush into long-term organizational goals and actions before you understand the "lay of the land."

- *Action Steps too vague.* Unless you know precisely what actions to take, as described in your Action Step, it will be impossible to evaluate success. For example, if your Action Step reads, "Be an effective leader to my teammates," you will be hard-pressed to assess your "effectiveness." What will it look like? How will you know when you've achieved it?

- *Being unwilling to modify your plan.* Realize things change and updates, edits and rewrites of Action Plans are quite common.
- *Keeping the plan quiet.* Share your plan with those who may provide you with ideas for embellishing or modifying it to make it more timely and relevant.
- *Getting buried in work.* In the rush to be an effective leader, many new leaders and managers find they are swallowed up in work (such as team duties, meetings, report writing, client meetings, strategy meetings, marketing meetings.) It's easy to finally look up, three to six months down the road, and find you haven't consulted your Action Plan and are behind in meeting the time frames you listed.

Personal Feedback Session

The SLA will conduct a personal feedback session with each participant. The purpose of the meeting is to share SLA observations, discuss follower reactions and seek participant reaction to the day's activities. Feedback is provided about progress throughout the course and during the day's leadership activity. The SLA also will share reactions of the follower group feedback session without disclosing individual follower identities.

The participant also will share reactions to the feedback and the leadership activity experience and provide the SLA with additional course feedback.

Completion of Certification Process

The SLA will assess and review the various components of the QLG Professional Leadership Certificate requirements including live instruction, on-the-job assignments, readings, Action Plan, Impact Paper and meeting certificate criteria.

Live Instruction: Discussions held between the participant and various QLG faculty members will be taken into consideration during the final certification evaluation process. Instructors will be asked to evaluate each participant on their leadership content mastery and their responses to success and failures of on-the-job applications.

On-the-Job Assignments: It is expected that participants complete all on-the-job assignments throughout the course and debrief their experiences with the SLA at the end of each week.

Discussions will illustrate commitment, continuous improvement, timeliness and integrity.

Readings: The SLA will discuss reading requirements as part of the weekly debriefing with each participant. It is expected all reading assignments will be completed and concepts discussed with the SLA and, as needed, with other QLG faculty members.

Action Plan: The SLA will assess and review the Action Plan of each participant for its relevancy, appropriateness and completeness.

Impact Paper: The Impact Paper is a document that allows participants to discuss, in written form, their thoughts on leadership; their new roles and responsibilities; and how the course has aided them in their quests to become effective leaders.

Meeting QLG Professional Leadership Certificate Criteria: Certification is based on the completion of all course requirements (including live instruction, readings, papers and assignments) and being evaluated successfully on the following criteria:

LEADERSHIP CONTENT MASTERY

Through on-the-job assignments and a site visit by the QLG Strategic Leadership Advisor, each participant will demonstrate in-depth knowledge of leadership concepts, models and tools, and how to apply them effectively in a work setting.

COMMITMENT

Through debriefings of readings and discussions of on-the-job leadership challenges, the participant will demonstrate to QLG faculty that he/she is physically, mentally and emotionally present when implementing leadership practices; takes leadership responsibilities seriously; and is committed to making the organization an effective, efficient and robust working environment.

CONTINUOUS IMPROVEMENT

Leaders recognize there is always a need for improvement, both in one's personal skills, knowledge and attitudes, and in organizational processes. The participant will show QLG faculty that he or she continually seeks ways to learn and apply leadership principles and practices through the development of an Action Plan, during live instruction discussions and in an Impact Paper.

INTEGRITY

To lead with integrity means telling the truth to others and oneself and acknowledging that personal reputation is the highest form of leadership influence. The participant will demonstrate Integrity in part through a confidential feedback session and through his/her responses to live instruction, on-the-job assignments and other interactions with QLG faculty.

TEAMWORK

Through the confidential feedback session and/or the experiential leadership practicum, the participant will demonstrate how effectively working with others, especially followers, is critical to the success of any individual, team, branch, division, department, organization—or leader.

OPENNESS

The participant shall demonstrate a willingness to speak freely and to seek the opinions and viewpoints of others, especially followers. This will be assessed by the QLG Strategic Leadership Advisor through the Action Plan the participant develops to implement leadership practices tailored to meet the needs of his/her organization.

EMPOWERMENT

A leader who "empowers" actively encourages and supports efforts of followers to take action on delegated tasks, especially when followers make mistakes. The Strategic Leadership Advisor will assess this criterion through a confidential feedback session with followers, through a review of Action Plans and an evaluation of Impact Papers.

TIMELINESS

Effective leaders work to reduce delays so deadlines and organizational goals can be met in a timely manner. Participants are expected to be punctual and fully attentive for all live instruction sessions and to complete assignments on time.

Recommendations for Continuous Learning: As a final site visit activity, the SLA will review and recommend a compendium of suggested readings, online courses and workshops, articles and other activities to aid each participant in the continuation of their leadership journeys.

SUMMARY

How does one lead into the future? Chapter One described a leader who, quite astutely, said he wouldn't know for many years if his decisions were correct or not. If that's the case, aren't all leadership decisions concerning individuals, teams, divisions, departments and even organizations potentially impactful?

New leaders have more learning resources and on-the-job opportunities to exhibit effective leadership practices than ever before. Leadership is more than a tyrannical boss screaming for employees to work harder. Those days, thankfully, are over. The task for new leaders is to identify which leadership practices are most effective. How much and to what extent should leaders get their hands dirty? How does fear of being wrong or being emotionally uncomfortable impact one's motivation and effort?

The Four Fatal Fears teaches that, in the extreme, fear can paralyze our ability to do anything. *Situational Leadership®II* tells us our leadership behaviors depend on the skills and attitudes of our followers. *The Leadership Challenge* tells us to "Model the Way" and act as a role model as we inspire our followers towards a vision of the future.

Yet *Servant Leadership* informs us that we must continually examine our motivation for leading. Are we motivated by the idea of obtaining the positional power we have always wanted (or lusted after), or is it about attaining a position that enables us to serve others? Could leadership be more than skills and knowledge and actually have something to do with heart and mind as well?

Emotional Intelligence teaches that leaders need to be aware of their emotions and recognize when they drive us towards making missteps and wrong decisions. *The Basic Elements® of Temperament* tells us that not only must we be aware of the dominant temperament of our personality, but we need to develop our other three temperaments too, especially our shadow temperament, to make us even better humans. Making matters even more difficult, the model informs us that we need to recognize that the temperament of our followers drives their behaviors just like ours does, and that leaders need to treat followers not as *we* want to be treated but how *they* want to be treated!

Moving forward, as we become clearer about the knowledge, skills and attitudes needed to become an effective leader, some tools and concepts are particularly helpful. Authors Cloke and Goldsmith teach us resolving conflicts at work can take up to 24 percent of our time and that we need to be able to understand the culture, dynamics and resistance that conflict brings to the workplace. *The Thomas-Kilmann Conflict Mode Instrument* provides us with insight into the five key methods of handling conflict and urges us to develop the two to three methods that are not our natural default approaches.

Authors Teresa de Grosbois and Karen Rowe remind us that to effectively influence followers, we must focus attention on critical organizational problems and not allow fear to prevent us from identifying and working with other key influencers while establishing organization-wide networks. QLG instructor Jim White suggests we can influence and direct teams and groups through the use of energetic questions, especially in moving away from the often negative criticism of past actions.

The building of trust between leaders and followers is absolutely essential for moving organizations toward a positive and successful future. QLG instructor Jeff Whitehead's *Results-Model* demonstrates we can easily misinterpret the behaviors of followers and coworkers that appear right before our eyes! Our Mind Maps need to be updated and well maintained in order to generate the best possible decision or action without jumping to conclusions.

Finally, the analysis of organizations by new leaders is a great way to rapidly understand and become more knowledgeable of hierarchies, committees, key issues and available resources. *The Organization as a System* model can be helpful in starting such an analysis, since organizational hierarchy alone will not capture the culture of a company.

Well-armed and equipped with leadership models, knowledge, concepts and tools, you now have everything you need to assume your new role and responsibilities with a level of confidence that will get you off to a good start. You are prepared to go forth into a future that will no doubt test your skills and patience. But don't forget, no matter how many models, concepts and tools you apply to all the situations you may encounter as a new leader, the *relationship* between leader and follower is what makes all the difference. Relationships are founded on a number of factors including trust, integrity, empathy and respect. Without growing, developing and nurturing these crucial elements, leadership doesn't happen.

"Only three things happen naturally in organizations: friction, confusion, and underperformance. Everything else requires leadership."

—Peter Drucker
Author & Management Consultant

At end of the fourth and final week of instruction, participants and readers connect again with their Strategic Leadership Advisor (SLA) or Coach/Mentor by phone or online and via an in-person visit by the SLA to their office. There may be more specific questions this week about leadership as participant and reader knowledge expands, and experience in applying leadership models and concepts on the job broadens. SLA/Coach/Mentor feedback discussion questions may include these samples:

- How would you describe your leadership performance in the activity you just led? What worked? What would you do differently?

- What leadership lessons do you believe are most important from each week of the course? Instruction? Assignments? Feedback discussions?

- What gaps remain in your understanding of leadership?

- What are highlights from your Action Plan for the next three, six and twelve months? What hurdles do you anticipate facing over the next year?

- Where do you want to go from here in your leadership learning? Courses? Workshops? Books? Podcasts? Webinars?

- The certification process includes an oral debriefing with the SLA and a paper describing how you view leadership and how you intend to apply leadership strategies on the job. Can you summarize your thoughts on the subject?

- What feedback do you have for us? Instructors? Materials? Content?

The following are sample assignments participants will complete by end of the fourth and final week of our program. The successes or remaining tasks from each assignment are discussed at the end of the week with the Strategic Leadership Advisor. Readers may hold this discussion with a coach or mentor.

Sample Assignments:

1. Arrange an activity for you to lead with your followers under the observation of your Strategic Leadership Advisor, Coach or Mentor.

2. Participate in a personal and confidential feedback session with your SLA about your leading a follower activity.

3. Review the highlights of your experience in completing all reading assignments. What major lessons have you learned?

4. Develop a detailed Action Plan outlining your leadership tasks and activities over the next three, six and twelve months.

5. Work with your SLA to identify additional leadership training courses, books and seminars to attend to further your leadership expertise.

6. Be ready to discuss how you rate your progress in becoming an effective leader.

7. Review this week's leadership instruction. What had the greatest impact on you? How might you utilize what you learned and apply it on the job?

8. Complete course certification requirements (including an Impact Paper describing how you view your leadership style and your plans for applying what you have learned on the job).

The following is a sample checklist that participants may be asked to complete by their fourth and final week of our program. Checklists are designed to remind participants of work that needs to be done during the week and provides a method for keeping track of their progress. The checklist may be reviewed and discussed at the end of the week with the Strategic Leadership Advisor/Coach/Mentor.

Sample Checklist Items:

1. Complete logistical arrangements for SLA site visit. ☐
2. Discuss feedback from actual leadership demonstration with the SLA. ☐
3. Identify lessons learned from the course. ☐
4. Complete an Action Plan for three, six and twelve months. ☐
5. Identify continuous leadership learning opportunities. ☐
6. Identify the most important lessons learned this week. ☐
7. Rate my leadership progress this week on a scale of 1 to 10. ☐
8. Complete course certification requirements. ☐

CHAPTER 6

QUICK LEADERSHIP 30-DAY GUIDE

The following is a guide that summarizes the key tasks new leaders and managers need to complete each day in order to maximize their effectiveness in 30 days. It's meant to be a short yet helpful guide to the various exercises, activities, readings, and tasks that participants are required to complete in the live "Quick! I Need to Be a Leader in 30 Days!" training course. Readers may use it as a blueprint for rapidly equipping themselves with a basic understanding of leadership and its practical application on the job.

HOW TO USE THIS GUIDE

This guide provides the reader with specific instructions for becoming an effective leader in only 30 days. Is this guidance all you need to be a successful leader? No. However, it's a great first step that enables new leaders to successfully handle leadership tasks during their first year in a leadership role.

> **Key Tasks & Activities:** These are suggested actions, presented in a graduated sequence, describing the activities that are presented and/or assigned as a part of the leadership training course. QLG instructors

provide online, live instruction two days per week. Topics for each session are identified in this 30-day guide. Readers may find additional information from readings and in the Reference Section of this book

Readings: These are books suggested to complement Key Tasks and Activities and discussions. It's anticipated that enrolled participants will complete all readings in a timely manner to enter into debriefing discussions with QLG instructors and the Strategic Leadership Advisor. Readers may obtain copies of these supplementary books and articles to enhance their own leadership training experience.

Comments: This section provides a narrative description of how instructional materials, debriefings, readings and homework assignments will be handled throughout the course. The learning focus is on specific participant applications of leadership principles on the job. Readers may implement any and all suggested activities and conduct debriefing sessions with mentors, coaches or supervisors.

The QLG faculty expects course participants to complete all activities and assignments on schedule, since learning modules build upon each subsequent session. Readers are urged to apply leadership practices and principles on the job, keep journals of their successes and complete all homework assignments.

"Management is efficiency in climbing a ladder of success; leadership determines whether the ladder is leaning against the right wall."

—STEPHEN COVEY
Author of "The 7 Habits of Highly Effective People"

QUICK LEADERSHIP GUIDE: PRE-WORK

KEY TASKS & ACTIVITIES

- REVIEW PRE-COURSE MATERIALS
- COMPLETE PERSONAL SKILLS CHALLENGES
- COMPLETE PERSONAL DEVELOPMENT CHALLENGES

READINGS

- *WHAT MAKES YOU TICK AND WHAT TICKS YOU OFF*

COMMENTS

Participants will prepare themselves for live instruction by completing several inventories (see Chapter One: Personal Skill Challenges and Personal Development Challenges) to begin the process of identifying existing strengths and skill areas to improve. It's expected that readers (and participants) ensure course content and discussions deal directly with the reinforcing of these strengths and the addressing of all issues.

In addition to the inventory assessments and weekly checklists, course participants also will receive a copy of, *Quick! I Need to Be a Leader in 30 Days!* Participants are expected to use this book as a guide and reference throughout the course. At times, instructional discussions and debriefings may refer to various sections in the book.

Participants are expected to be ready to discuss their views on leadership and their own thoughts about becoming an effective leader on Day 1.

> *"Power in organizations is the capacity generated by relationships. It is an energy that comes into existence through relationships."*
>
> —MARGARET J. WHEATLEY
> *American Writer & Organization Behavior Consultant*

QUICK LEADERSHIP GUIDE: DAY 1

KEY TASKS & ACTIVITIES

- COURSE ORIENTATION
- REVIEW OF PRE-ASSESSMENT INFORMATION
- PARTICIPANT READINESS FOR LEADERSHIP
- ONLINE LIVE PRESENTATION/DISCUSSION ON LEADERSHIP VS. MANAGEMENT
- ONLINE LIVE PRESENTATION/DISCUSSION ON TYPES OF LEADERSHIP POWER
- ONLINE LIVE PRESENTATION/DISCUSSION ON THE FOUR FATAL FEARS

READINGS

- *WHAT MAKES YOU TICK AND WHAT TICKS YOU OFF*

COMMENTS

The first day of the "Quick! I Need to Be a Leader in 30 Days!" certificate course focuses on the results of pre-course inventories and initial course orientation during live online discussions with a QLG instructor.

There are two live instruction sessions scheduled. The first presentation and discussion will focus on participant readiness to become a leader. This is an opportunity to freely share thoughts on personal strengths, fears and excitement for becoming an effective leader and assuming a new or expanded role in the organization.

The second session will focus on differences between leadership and management as well as a review of the three types of power in organizations. The session also reviews the Four Fatal Fears and their potential impact on leadership. Participants are expected to disclose the personal fears they experience or anticipate feeling about their new leadership roles.

Both sessions are interactive, and participants are expected to fully disclose their reactions, ideas and concerns about the subject matter. The QLG instructor also will present the concept of applying leadership principles and practices through on-the-job homework assignments and provide examples to tailor the assignments to meet the needs of the participant's organization.

Finally, homework assignments (see Chapter One: Week 1 Assignments and Week 1 Checklist) will be made, and the scheduled Day 5 debriefing with the Strategic Leadership Advisor is reviewed.

> "Leadership is the capacity to translate vision into reality."
>
> —WARREN G. BENNIS
> *Author and Organizational Consultant*

QUICK LEADERSHIP GUIDE: DAY 2

KEY TASKS & ACTIVITIES

- ONLINE LIVE PRESENTATION/DISCUSSION ON THE BASIC ELEMENTS® OF TEMPERAMENT
- ON-THE-JOB ASSIGNMENTS

READINGS

- *WHAT MAKES YOU TICK AND WHAT TICKS YOU OFF* (CONTINUED)

COMMENTS

The second day of instruction includes two live sessions, both of which focus on introducing the *Basic Elements of Temperament* model. Participants will identify their dominant and shadow temperaments and discuss how this knowledge can help them become more aware and sensitive to the needs of their followers. Depending on how much they've read on the subject, the QLG instructor will incorporate participant knowledge into the discussion, as appropriate.

Participants are expected to continue their reading assignment and begin to apply what they've learned in on-the-job situations. For example, participants may be asked to identify where a fatal fear is at play on a team, division or department.

All participants will be asked to keep a journal or record of their reactions, observations and any leadership questions that arise. These journals will be a vital resource for personal reflection and serve as a resource for debriefings with the Strategic Leadership Advisor throughout the program.

> *"Leadership is a relationship between those who aspire to lead and those who choose to follow."*
>
> —JAMES. M. KOUZES
> *Coauthor of "The Leadership Challenge"*

QUICK LEADERSHIP GUIDE: DAY 3

KEY TASKS & ACTIVITIES

- REVIEW OF DAY 1 AND DAY 2 LESSONS LEARNED
- ON-THE-JOB OBSERVATIONS: FOUR FATAL FEARS
- ON-THE-JOB OBSERVATIONS: BASIC ELEMENTS® OF TEMPERAMENT
- KEEP A JOURNAL OF REACTIONS/LEADERSHIP ISSUES

READINGS

- *WHAT MAKES YOU TICK AND WHAT TICKS YOU OFF* (CONTINUED)

During the third day of instruction, participants are expected to focus on on-the-job applications of what they've learned and read from Day 1 and Day 2. For example, participants may observe how management and leadership behaviors differ. They may identify the types of fear they observe in followers. They also may identify the dominant temperaments of key followers or executives and locate leadership power in the organization.

Participants are expected to continue their reading assignment and make regular journal entries. Journals are confidential and used only to record personal growth, capture reactions, and note leadership questions. On course Day 30, participants will review what they've written to assess personal growth and leadership improvement.

Participants also are encouraged to identify additional leadership articles and/or news items they wish to discuss with a QLG instructor or the Strategic Leadership Advisor (SLA).

> *"Power is like being a lady. . . . If you have to tell people you are, you aren't."*
>
> —MARGARET THATCHER
> *Former British Prime Minister*

QUICK LEADERSHIP GUIDE: DAY 4

KEY TASKS & ACTIVITIES

- REVIEW OF DAY 1 AND DAY 2 LESSONS LEARNED
- ON-THE-JOB OBSERVATIONS: FOUR FATAL FEARS
- ON-THE-JOB OBSERVATIONS: BASIC ELEMENTS® OF TEMPERAMENT
- JOURNALING

READINGS

- *WHAT MAKES YOU TICK AND WHAT TICKS YOU OFF*
  (CONTINUED)

COMMENTS

During the fourth day of instruction, participants are expected to focus on additional on-the-job applications of course content. Observations of the Four Fatal Fears, temperament and leadership power examples reinforce the Day 1 and Day 2 concepts and serve to make instructional leadership models more real and relevant.

It's also expected that participants spend a few minutes reviewing journal entries. Journaling is a very free-form assignment, and many participants use drawings, bullet points, keywords, and diagrams to be reminded of individual observations and questions about a particular leadership subject.

Reading assignments continue, and participants are urged to make notes for later discussions with their Strategic Leadership Advisor (SLA) on Day 5 or with a QLG instructor during Week 2. Checklists and other assignments continue in preparation for discussion with the SLA.

> *"Leadership should be born out of the understanding of the needs of those who would be affected by it."*
>
> —MARION ANDERSON
> *Contralto & Opera Star*

QUICK LEADERSHIP GUIDE: DAY 5

KEY TASKS & ACTIVITIES

- ONLINE LIVE DEBRIEFING WITH STRATEGIC LEADERSHIP ADVISOR (SLA)/COACH OR MENTOR
- REVIEW OF CHECKLIST

- REVIEW OF HOMEWORK ASSIGNMENTS
- JOURNALING

READINGS

- *LEADERSHIP AND THE ONE MINUTE MANAGER*
- *THE LEADERSHIP CHALLENGE*
- *WHAT MAKES YOU TICK AND WHAT TICKS YOU OFF* (CONTINUED)

COMMENTS

The fifth day of instruction includes a one-hour online, live discussion with the Strategic Leadership Advisor (SLA). The SLA (see Chapter Five: Role of the Strategic Leadership Advisor) will complete the following:

- Lead a weekly debriefing session with the participant
- Facilitate a discussion on the impact of that week's live instruction
- Answer participant journal questions
- Review participant checklists
- Review and discuss the week's on-the-job assignments
- Discuss the week's reading assignment
- Assign new reading books

Of particular interest to the SLA are participant observations and on-the-job applications of leadership course content. The SLA will discuss readings for the week and link leadership concepts in the book to practical applications attempted by participants in the workplace. Participants are expected to offer their thoughts on how to deal with followers who experience one or more of the Four Fatal Fears. They're also expected to discuss how and where they see potential temperament differences in their team, department or organization.

The SLA answers participant questions from Day 1 and Day 2 topics including temperament, the Four Fatal Fears and the three types of power. The SLA also may refer questions to other QLG faculty members for a response. Participants are expected to complete checklist items and identify and discuss difficulties they experienced while completing them.

The SLA also discusses the participant's use of a journal. For many, maintaining a journal is time-consuming and of questionable value. However the SLA asks participants to consider that reflection and evaluation of personal efforts are important aspects of effective leadership training.

Finally, the SLA assigns new reading books for Week 2.

> *"The leaders who work most effectively, it seems to me, never say 'I.' And that's not because they have trained themselves not to say 'I.' They don't think 'I.' They think 'we'; they think 'team.' They understand their job to be to make the team function. They accept responsibility and don't sidestep it, but 'we' gets the credit. This is what creates trust, what enables you to get the task done."*
>
> —PETER DRUCKER
> *Author and Management Consultant*

QUICK LEADERSHIP GUIDE: DAY 6

KEY TASKS & ACTIVITIES

- REVIEW OF SLA DEBRIEFING
- CONTINUE READING
- JOURNALING

READINGS

- *LEADERSHIP AND THE ONE MINUTE MANAGER* (CONTINUED)
- *THE LEADERSHIP CHALLENGE* (CONTINUED)
- *WHAT MAKES YOU TICK AND WHAT TICKS YOU OFF* (CONTINUED)

COMMENTS

During the sixth day of instruction, participants spend time reviewing the results of the SLA debriefing during Day 5, reflecting on what they've accomplished during the first course week, and writing their reactions in journals.

Based on their journaling and on-the-job experiences during Week 1, participants are expected to develop questions for QLG instructors in preparation for live sessions on Day 8 and Day 9.

> *"I suppose leadership at one time meant muscles; but today it means getting along with people."*
>
> —MAHATMA GANDHI
> *Father of the Nation of India*

QUICK LEADERSHIP GUIDE: DAY 7

KEY TASKS & ACTIVITIES

- REVIEW OF SLA DEBRIEFING
- CONTINUE READING
- JOURNALING

READINGS

- *LEADERSHIP AND THE ONE MINUTE MANAGER* (CONTINUED)

- *THE LEADERSHIP CHALLENGE* (CONTINUED)
- *WHAT MAKES YOU TICK AND WHAT TICKS YOU OFF* (CONTINUED)

COMMENTS

The seventh day of instruction is similar to Day 6 in that it's a day devoted to leadership reading and reflection and analysis of the Day 1 and Day 2 live instruction, journaling, on-the-job observations, homework activities, checklists and the SLA debriefing on Day 5.

Participants are expected to continue reading two new leadership books that provide practical steps for new leaders to develop better relationships with followers. These classic leadership volumes are tailored for those developing basic strategies for successfully assuming new leadership roles.

Participants are expected to identify questions and/or concerns they may have in preparation for their Day 12 SLA debriefing. Leadership concepts from the two new books will be presented during the Day 8 and Day 9 live sessions.

> *"People ask the difference between a leader and a boss. The leader leads, and the boss drives."*
>
> —THEODORE ROOSEVELT
> *26th U.S. President*

QUICK LEADERSHIP GUIDE: DAY 8

KEY TASKS & ACTIVITIES

- ONLINE LIVE INSTRUCTION OF *SITUATIONAL LEADERSHIP®II*
- ONLINE LIVE INSTRUCTION OF *THE FIVE PRACTICES OF EXEMPLARY LEADERSHIP*

- JOURNALING

READINGS

- *LEADERSHIP AND THE ONE MINUTE MANAGER* (CONTINUED)
- *THE LEADERSHIP CHALLENGE* (CONTINUED)

COMMENTS

The eighth day of instruction includes live instruction on two critical leadership models. The first session's presentation and discussion will focus on *Situational Leadership®II*. Developed by Ken Blanchard and the founding associates of The Ken Blanchard Companies, this model explores the relationship between the leader and the skills and personal commitment of the follower required to complete a task.

The second session may continue the earlier presentation and discussion on *Situational Leadership®II* and/or introduce *The Five Practices of Exemplary Leadership*. Based on the assigned leadership book, *The Leadership Challenge*, this model provides specific actions a new leader can take to provide followers with effective leadership.

Participants are advised to continue their readings and use their journals to record observations, questions and remaining leadership concerns. New checklists and homework assignments are made, and tasks this week are directly related to all the new leadership approaches presented.

> *"If your actions inspire others to dream more, learn more, do more and become more, you are a leader."*
>
> —JOHN QUINCY ADAMS
> *6th U.S. President*

QUICK LEADERSHIP GUIDE: DAY 9

KEY TASKS & ACTIVITIES

- ONLINE LIVE INSTRUCTION OF *SERVANT LEADERSHIP*
- ONLINE LIVE INSTRUCTION OF STAGES OF TEAM DEVELOPMENT
- JOURNALING

READINGS

- *LEADERSHIP AND THE ONE MINUTE MANAGER*
- (CONTINUED)
- *THE LEADERSHIP CHALLENGE* (CONTINUED)

COMMENTS

The ninth day of instruction starts with completion of discussions on *Situational Leadership®II* and/or *The Five Practices of Exemplary Leadership*. These models provide participants with knowledge, skills and specific actions they can take to understand follower motivation.

The remaining time of the first session and the entire second session will focus on introducing the leadership concept of *Servant Leadership* as well as Bruce Tuckman's *Stages of Group Development* model.

Servant Leadership presents the "leader-first" vs. "servant-first" dichotomy and asks participants to analyze and discuss benefits of each. The Tuckman model helps new leaders analyze and diagnose team progress in completing a task or assignment or achieving a goal. Examples provided will illustrate the applications of both Tuckman and *Servant Leadership*.

It should be noted that during this second week of the course, it's critically important readers and participants identify specific issues and/or problems they're facing or anticipate in their new leadership positions. These concerns are discussed with QLG instructors, the SLA, coaches or mentors.

Readers and participants are advised to continue their journaling efforts to reflect on personal reactions to course topics, checklists, readings, and on-the-job assignments. It cannot be stressed enough that personal reflection is a key element in the success of an effective leader.

> "The Servant-Leader is servant first. . . . It begins with the natural feeling that one wants to serve, to serve first. Then conscious choice brings one to aspire to lead. That person is sharply different from one who is leader first."
>
> —ROBERT K. GREENLEAF
> Founder, Servant Leadership Movement

QUICK LEADERSHIP GUIDE: DAY 10

KEY TASKS & ACTIVITIES

- REVIEW OF DAY 8 AND DAY 9 LESSONS LEARNED
- ON-THE-JOB OBSERVATIONS: SITUATIONAL LEADERSHIP
- ON-THE-JOB OBSERVATIONS: FIVE PRACTICES OF EXEMPLARY LEADERSHIP
- ON-THE-JOB OBSERVATIONS: STAGES OF GROUP DEVELOPMENT
- JOURNALING

READINGS

- *LEADERSHIP AND THE ONE MINUTE MANAGER* (CONTINUED)
- *THE LEADERSHIP CHALLENGE* (CONTINUED)

187

COMMENTS

During the 10th day of instruction, QLG faculty members expect readers and participants to work on their checklists, readings and completing on-the-job assignments.

Today's focus is on observing and applying *Situational Leadership®II* and *The Five Practices of Exemplary Leadership* on the job. Readers and participants are encouraged to record examples of both models they observe in their journals.

Participants are also expected to observe group and team development and effectiveness using the Tuckman model as well as continue to observe leadership power at play and note examples of organizational fear. Participants are expected to continue working on weekly checklists and assignments and be prepared to discuss them during their Day 12 SLA sessions.

"We herd sheep, we drive cattle, we lead people. Lead me, follow me, or get out of my way."

—GEORGE S. PATTON
Former U.S. General

QUICK LEADERSHIP GUIDE: DAY 11

KEY TASKS & ACTIVITIES

- REVIEW OF DAY 8 AND DAY 9 LESSONS LEARNED
- ON-THE-JOB OBSERVATIONS: SITUATIONAL LEADERSHIP
- ON-THE-JOB OBSERVATIONS: FIVE PRACTICES OF EXEMPLARY LEADERSHIP
- ON-THE-JOB OBSERVATIONS: STAGES OF GROUP DEVELOPMENT
- JOURNALING

- *LEADERSHIP AND THE ONE MINUTE MANAGER* (CONTINUED)
- *THE LEADERSHIP CHALLENGE* (CONTINUED)

COMMENTS

The 11th day of instruction again provides participants with opportunities to apply what they've learned in on-the-job situations. Focus continues on the observation of behaviors and other activities related to *Situational Leadership®II, The Five Practices of Exemplary Leadership*, and team development.

Journaling is strongly encouraged to record personal reactions, questions and any and all leadership topics unaddressed to date. A review of these topics and participant reactions will take place during the Day 12 SLA session or, for readers, with their coaches or mentors.

Additional materials may be provided or referred to in preparation for live instruction on Day 15 and Day 16 on the topics of Emotional Intelligence and Conflict Management.

> *"The task of the leader is to get his people from where they are to where they have not been."*
>
> —Henry A. Kissinger
> *Former U.S. Secretary of State*

QUICK LEADERSHIP GUIDE: DAY 12

KEY TASKS & ACTIVITIES

- ONLINE LIVE DEBRIEFING WITH STRATEGIC LEADERSHIP ADVISOR (SLA)/COACH OR MENTOR
- REVIEW OF CHECKLIST

- REVIEW OF HOMEWORK
- JOURNALING

READINGS

- *LEADERSHIP: THE POWER OF EMOTIONAL INTELLIGENCE—SELECTED WRITINGS*
- *RESOLVING CONFLICTS AT WORK: TEN STRATEGIES FOR EVERYONE ON THE JOB*
- *THOMAS-KILMANN CONFLICT MANAGEMENT MODE INSTRUMENT*

COMMENTS

The 12th day of instruction includes the second online discussion with the Strategic Leadership Advisor (SLA). The SLA will expect to ask for personal reactions to this week's live instruction, observations at work, checklists, assignments and lessons learned from readings. Readers may conduct similar sessions with coaches/mentors.

Of particular interest are participant observations of *Situational Leadership®II*, *The Five Practices of Exemplary Leadership*, and team development. The expectation is for participants to cite examples of when they have observed these leadership models at play in their organizations and when they personally tried to apply them.

Participants also are asked about readings for the week, and new books are assigned. It's acknowledged participants can easily fall behind on their required reading list. The SLA expects to remind participants of the importance of completing the readings in a timely manner, as well as making daily journal entries.

"Whenever you're in conflict with someone there is one factor that can make the difference between damaging your relationship and deepening it. That factor is attitude."

—WILLIAM JAMES
American Philosopher

QUICK LEADERSHIP GUIDE: DAY 13

KEY TASKS & ACTIVITIES

- REVIEW OF SLA DEBRIEFING
- KEEP READING
- JOURNALING

READINGS

- *LEADERSHIP: THE POWER OF EMOTIONAL INTELLIGENCE—SELECTED WRITINGS* (CONTINUED)
- *RESOLVING CONFLICTS AT WORK: TEN STRATEGIES FOR EVERYONE ON THE JOB* (CONTINUED)
- *TKI CONFLICT MANAGEMENT MODE INSTRUMENT* (CONTINUED)

COMMENTS

The 13th day of instruction focuses on the review of the SLA debriefing. Participants are expected to follow up with agreed-upon tasks and activities. Readers may do the same from agreed-upon tasks with their coaches or mentors.

Participants are expected to continue reading new leadership books to prepare them for live instruction during the Day 15 and 16 sessions.

Today's focus also is on reflection and analysis of journal entries. Based on their journaling, participants develop questions for

QLG instructors and/or the SLA and identify potential on-the-job leadership applications for Week 3.

> *"As women's leadership qualities come to play a more dominant role in the public sphere, their particular aptitudes for long-term negotiating, analytic listening and creating an ambiance in which people work with zest and spirit will help reconcile the split between the ideals of being efficient and being humane. This integration of female values is already producing a more collaborative kind of leadership, and changing the very ideal of what strong leadership actually is."*
>
> —Sally Helgesen
> Author of "The Female Advantage:
> Women's Ways of Leadership"

QUICK LEADERSHIP GUIDE: DAY 14

KEY TASKS & ACTIVITIES

- REVIEW OF SLA DEBRIEFING
- KEEP READING
- JOURNALING

READINGS

- *LEADERSHIP: THE POWER OF EMOTIONAL INTELLIGENCE— SELECTED WRITINGS* (CONTINUED)
- *RESOLVING CONFLICTS AT WORK: TEN STRATEGIES FOR EVERYONE ON THE JOB* (CONTINUED)
- *THOMAS-KILMANN CONFLICT MANAGEMENT MODE INSTRUMENT* (CONTINUED)

COMMENTS

The 14th day of instruction continues participant examination and review of results after the Day 12 debriefing by the Strategic Leadership Advisor (SLA). Participants are expected to work on checklist items and complete homework assignments. Readers may do the same based on their conversations with coaches or mentors.

Participants also are expected to continue reading their new leadership books to prepare them for live instruction during the Day 15 and 16 sessions.

In addition to completing homework activities and readings, participants are reminded to reflect and analyze journal entries in order to develop questions for QLG instructors and the SLA for the Day 19 session.

> "Be a yardstick of quality. Some people aren't used to an environment where excellence is expected."
>
> —STEVE JOBS
> Entrepreneur

QUICK LEADERSHIP GUIDE: DAY 15

KEY TASKS & ACTIVITIES

- ONLINE LIVE PRESENTATION ON EMOTIONAL INTELLIGENCE
- ONLINE LIVE PRESENTATION ON FOUR ENERGETIC DIRECTIONS OF QUESTIONS
- ONLINE LIVE PRESENTATION ON CONFLICT MANAGEMENT
- JOURNALING

READINGS

- *LEADERSHIP: THE POWER OF EMOTIONAL INTELLIGENCE— SELECTED WRITINGS* (CONTINUED)

- *RESOLVING CONFLICTS AT WORK: TEN STRATEGIES FOR EVERYONE ON THE JOB* (CONTINUED)
- *TKI CONFLICT MANAGEMENT MODE INSTRUMENT* (CONTINUED)

COMMENTS

The 15th day (and halfway point in the course) of instruction focuses on the introduction of several leadership models that provide participants and readers with knowledge and skills in dealing with followers, teams and organizations from an interpersonal perspective. The first session presents *Emotional Intelligence* as a model and, depending on time, *The Four Energetic Directions of Questions*. The second session focuses on conflict management, including the *TKI Conflict Management Mode Instrument*.

Readings will continue, and journals used to record observations, reactions and remaining leadership concerns. New checklists and on-the-job assignments will be made and participants are expected to suggest tailored homework assignments that meet specific needs of their organizations.

> "The insight to see possible new paths, the courage to try them, the judgment to measure results—these are the qualities of a leader."
>
> —MARY PARKER FOLLETT
> *Pioneer in Organizational Theory*

QUICK LEADERSHIP GUIDE: DAY 15 (OPTIONAL PRACTICUM)

KEY TASKS & ACTIVITIES

- OFF-SITE LIVE PRACTICUM

- OFF-SITE EXPERIENTIAL EXERCISES
- PRESENTATION OF THE "RESULTS-MODEL"
- PRESENTATION OF ORGANIZATIONAL CULTURE & INFLUENCE
- JOURNALING

READINGS

- *LEADERSHIP: THE POWER OF EMOTIONAL INTELLIGENCE—SELECTED WRITINGS* (CONTINUED)
- *RESOLVING CONFLICTS AT WORK: TEN STRATEGIES FOR EVERYONE ON THE JOB* (CONTINUED)
- *TKI CONFLICT MANAGEMENT MODE INSTRUMENT* (CONTINUED)

COMMENTS

OPTIONAL: For organizations enrolling eight or more participants, a two-day, optional, off-site session is offered in Maryland or Florida (or alternate location). The first instructional day includes presentations on the Results-Model and an introduction to organizational culture and influence. These models provide templates for decision-making and successfully influencing people and organizations.

Participants spend the rest of the day working individually and in teams solving physical and mental challenges, such as puzzles, ropes and other outdoor adventure tasks. These activities are designed to build trust, self-confidence and team spirit.

Participants continue journaling to identify leadership issues they face or expect to face in their new positions. A review of these issues is scheduled for the Day 19 session with the SLA.

"Leaders are not born, they're made."

—VINCE LOMBARDI
Hall of Fame Football Coach

QUICK LEADERSHIP GUIDE: DAY 16

KEY TASKS & ACTIVITIES

- ONLINE LIVE PRESENTATION OF THE "RESULTS-MODEL"
- ONLINE LIVE PRESENTATION OF THE "ORGANIZATION AS A SYSTEM" MODEL
- ONLINE PRESENTATION OF ORGANIZATIONAL INFLUENCE & CHANGE
- JOURNALING

READINGS

- *LEADERSHIP: THE POWER OF EMOTIONAL INTELLIGENCE— SELECTED WRITINGS* (CONTINUED)
- *RESOLVING CONFLICTS AT WORK: TEN STRATEGIES FOR EVERYONE ON THE JOB* (CONTINUED)
- *TKI CONFLICT MANAGEMENT MODE INSTRUMENT* (CONTINUED)

COMMENTS

The 16th day of instruction includes presentations and discussions on how new leaders view and effectively lead their organizations. The first session explores the Results-Model as a decision-making tool and construct. Another model, Organization as a System, depicts how new leaders can analyze their organizations by exploring four overlapping sectors: Technical, Administrative, Strategic and Social.

The second session explores how one person can influence others in an organization. Discussions are held to respond to participant questions, reactions and strategies related to practical applications of all leadership concepts and models on the job.

"Success isn't about how much money you make; it's about the difference you make in people's lives."

—MICHELLE OBAMA
Former First Lady of the U.S.

QUICK LEADERSHIP GUIDE: DAY 16 (OPTIONAL PRACTICUM)

KEY TASKS & ACTIVITIES

- OFF-SITE EXPERIENTIAL EXERCISES
- PRESENTATION OF THE "ORGANIZATION AS A SYSTEM" MODEL
- PRESENTATION OF ORGANIZATIONAL INFLUENCE
- JOURNALING

READINGS

- *LEADERSHIP: THE POWER OF EMOTIONAL INTELLIGENCE— SELECTED WRITINGS* (CONTINUED)
- *RESOLVING CONFLICTS AT WORK: TEN STRATEGIES FOR EVERYONE ON THE JOB* (CONTINUED)
- *TKI CONFLICT MANAGEMENT MODE INSTRUMENT* (CONTINUED)

COMMENTS

OPTIONAL: The second day of the optional practicum continues the off-site, experiential activities that build trust, self-confidence and team development.

Today's session includes a presentation on the *Organization as a System* model and continues the discussion on successfully influencing people and the organization. As in Day 15 of the optional course, participants spend most of the day working on outdoor activities that tests them physically and mentally. After the completion of each activity, the QLG instructor will lead a debriefing session to discuss the leadership lessons learned.

Ample time will be devoted for participants to work together to share experiences and discuss some of the leadership models, tools and concepts they've learned so far in the course. The QLG instructor will be available to answer questions and clarify any of the previous coursework.

"Leadership and learning are indispensable to each other."

—JOHN F. KENNEDY
35th U.S. President

QUICK LEADERSHIP GUIDE: DAY 17

KEY TASKS & ACTIVITIES

- ON-THE-JOB APPLICATIONS: EMOTIONAL INTELLIGENCE
- ON-THE-JOB APPLICATIONS: CONFLICT MANAGEMENT
- ON-THE-JOB APPLICATIONS: ORGANIZATION AS A SYSTEM
- ON-THE-JOB APPLICATIONS: ORGANIZATIONAL INFLUENCE
- ON-THE-JOB APPLICATIONS: RESULTS-MODEL
- KEEP READING
- JOURNALING

READINGS

- *LEADERSHIP: THE POWER OF EMOTIONAL INTELLIGENCE— SELECTED WRITINGS* (CONTINUED)
- *RESOLVING CONFLICTS AT WORK: TEN STRATEGIES FOR EVERYONE ON THE JOB* (CONTINUED)
- *TKI CONFLICT MANAGEMENT MODE INSTRUMENT* (CONTINUED)

COMMENTS

The 17th day of instruction combines a number of concepts and models for participants and readers to observe and apply on the job. They're encouraged to record personal reactions and questions in their journals. Homework assignments focus on analyzing the internal operations of organizations as well as the development of influencing strategies.

Participants and readers are expected to identify organizational approaches to mass influence and identify key players for potential networking contacts.

Conflict management techniques, particularly the *TKI Conflict Management Mode Instrument* and Cloke and Goldsmith's *Resolving Conflicts at Work: Ten Strategies for Everyone On The Job*, are used to identify the most common organizational modes of handling conflict.

> *"The only safe ship in a storm is leadership."*
>
> —FAYE WATTLETON
> *American Author and former CEO*

QUICK LEADERSHIP GUIDE: DAY 18

KEY TASKS & ACTIVITIES

- ON-THE-JOB APPLICATIONS: EMOTIONAL INTELLIGENCE
- ON-THE-JOB APPLICATIONS: CONFLICT MANAGEMENT
- ON-THE-JOB APPLICATIONS: ORGANIZATION AS A SYSTEM
- ON-THE-JOB APPLICATIONS: ORGANIZATIONAL INFLUENCE
- ON-THE-JOB APPLICATIONS: RESULTS-MODEL
- KEEP READING
- JOURNALING

READINGS

- *LEADERSHIP: THE POWER OF EMOTIONAL INTELLIGENCE— SELECTED WRITINGS* (CONTINUED)

- *RESOLVING CONFLICTS AT WORK: TEN STRATEGIES FOR EVERYONE ON THE JOB* (CONTINUED)
- *TKI CONFLICT MANAGEMENT MODE INSTRUMENT* (CONTINUED)

COMMENTS

The 18th day of instruction provides participants and readers with an opportunity to make on-the-job observations and applications of the leadership models, tools and concepts presented during Day 15 and Day 16.

Today, the focus is on observations of organizational approaches, practices and procedures for dealing with conflict, attaining influence and enhancing personal decision-making. Participants and readers are encouraged to record their reactions and questions in their journals and make every effort to analyze corporate culture and identify potential influencing strategies.

> *"Leadership is understanding people and involving them to help you do a job. That takes all of the good characteristics, like integrity, dedication of purpose, selflessness, knowledge, skill, implacability, as well as determination not to accept failure."*
>
> —ARLEIGH BURKE
> *Former Admiral, U.S. Navy*

QUICK LEADERSHIP GUIDE: DAY 19

KEY TASKS & ACTIVITIES

- ONLINE LIVE DEBRIEFING WITH STRATEGIC LEADERSHIP ADVISOR (SLA)/COACH OR MENTOR
- REVIEW OF CHECKLIST

- REVIEW OF HOMEWORK ASSIGNMENTS
- KEEP READING
- JOURNALING

READINGS

- *MASS INFLUENCE: THE HABITS OF THE HIGHLY INFLUENTIAL*

COMMENTS

The 19th day of instruction includes the third online discussion with the Strategic Leadership Advisor (SLA) concerning the week's activities. The SLA expects to ask for personal reactions to live instruction, observations, checklists, on-the-job assignments and lessons learned from readings.

Since the past week included a number of leadership models, tools and concepts related to the organization, the SLA anticipates participant examples of when and how these leadership practices appear on the job. It's expected that participants find some tools and concepts more useful than others. The SLA is specifically interested in participant observations concerning such topics as Emotional Intelligence, the Results-Model, organizational influence and conflict management.

The SLA also assigns a new reading book; reviews the Week 3 agenda; and answers questions about the logistics necessary for the Day 30 Site Visit.

> *"I like to take chances on people, and whenever possible, promote from within—it sends a great message to everyone in the company when someone demonstrates a passion for the job and leadership skills at every step along the way and is rewarded with a leadership role."*
>
> —RICHARD BRANSON
> *British Business Magnate*

QUICK LEADERSHIP GUIDE: DAY 20

KEY TASKS & ACTIVITIES

- REVIEW OF SLA DEBRIEFING
- KEEP READING
- JOURNALING

READINGS

- *MASS INFLUENCE: THE HABITS OF THE HIGHLY INFLUENTIAL* (CONTINUED)

COMMENTS

The 20th day of instruction will afford readers and participants the opportunity to review the results of their Day 19 SLA/Coach/ Mentor debriefing sessions. The reading assignment continues, and readers and participants reflect on their progress to date as well as reactions to course content, checklists and on-the- job assignments.

As the course winds down to its final 10 days, it's of increasingly critical importance to maintain journals to record observations, concerns and remaining questions about specific leadership topics.

Today's focus is on identifying the most influential employees in the organization and examining the source of their influence. Is it their reputation, experience, longevity, Position Power or something completely different that makes them so influential?

> *"Example is not the main thing in influencing others. It is the only thing."*
>
> —ALBERT SCHWEITZER
> *Nobel Peace Prize Winner, 1952*

QUICK LEADERSHIP GUIDE: DAY 21

KEY TASKS & ACTIVITIES

- REVIEW OF SLA DEBRIEFING
- CONTINUE READING
- JOURNALING

READINGS

- *MASS INFLUENCE: THE HABITS OF THE HIGHLY INFLUENTIAL* (CONTINUED)

COMMENTS

The 21st day of instruction focuses readers and participants on the completion of weekly activities, checklists and assignments. Participants also are expected to complete any agreed-upon tasks and activities discussed with the SLA during the Day 19 debriefing session. Readers may do the same with agreements made with coaches or mentors.

Participants also are expected to continue reading about mass influence and reflect upon lessons learned. The focus today is exploring how the most influential employees exert their influence throughout the organization. Do they hold brown bag lunches or write a website blog? Conversations with such employees can reveal a number of successful techniques, methods and procedures.

Based on their journal entries and reflections, it's anticipated participants develop questions for QLG instructors in preparation for the Day 22 and 23 live sessions.

> *"A leader . . . is like a shepherd. He stays behind the flock, letting the most nimble go out ahead, whereupon the others follow, not realizing that all along, they are being directed from behind."*
>
> —NELSON MANDELA
> *Former South African President*

QUICK LEADERSHIP GUIDE: DAY 22

KEY TASKS & ACTIVITIES

- ONLINE LIVE PRESENTATION/DISCUSSION ON ENVISIONING A LEADERSHIP FUTURE
- ONLINE LIVE PRESENTATION/DISCUSSION ON ACTION PLANNING

READINGS

- CONTINUATION OF ALL REQUIRED READING

COMMENTS

The 22nd day (fourth week) of instruction includes two live sessions with a QLG faculty member. This week's focus, "Leading Into the Future," calls for readers and participants to reflect on what they've learned about leadership and imagine what their future may portend about their success.

The first session today focuses on the future. Participants are guided through an exercise asking them to think back over the past three weeks, then imagine up to a year into the future. They will identify key hurdles they've overcome, as well as successes they achieved.

The second session introduces an *Action Planning* model and template for readers and participants to specifically identify the steps they'll take over the next three-, six- and 12-month periods to become more effective leaders.

While many texts on the subject of "Action Planning" advise waiting a year or so to ensure organizational understanding before contemplating—let alone completing—a specific Action Plan, course participants will develop three plans focusing on their post-course development of leadership skills, knowledge and attitudes.

"Leadership can't be claimed like luggage at the airport. Leadership can't be inherited, even though you may inherit a leadership position. . . . Leadership must be earned by mastering a defined set of skills and by working with others to achieve common goals."

—DAVID COTTRELL
Award-Winning Leadership Expert

QUICK LEADERSHIP GUIDE: DAY 23

KEY TASKS & ACTIVITIES

- ONLINE LIVE PRESENTATION/DISCUSSION ON COURSE CERTIFICATION PROCESS
- ONLINE LIVE MAKE-UP SESSION, AS NEEDED
- LOGISTICAL REQUIREMENTS FOR SITE VISIT
- CHECKLISTS/ASSIGNMENTS

READINGS

- CONTINUATION OF ALL REQUIRED READING

COMMENTS

The 23rd day of instruction will review the certification process for the course and provide participants with an opportunity to revisit any previous leadership module. It's anticipated there are a number of comments and questions about the Action Plan, the final course certification requirements and previous instructional sessions.

The first session reviews the remaining tasks needed to obtain a QLG Professional Leadership Certificate. These requirements include:

- Completion of an Impact Paper
- Site Visit by the SLA

– SLA observation of a Leadership Task

– Completion of the Action Plan

The Impact Paper is a three- to five-page document requiring participants to describe in narrative form what they have gained from the course and how they intend to apply what they've learned on the job. The Impact Paper may be submitted to the SLA prior to or during the Site Visit.

The one-day SLA site visit (Day 30) includes an observation of an activity led by the participant to demonstrate a leadership skill. The specific activity will be determined by each participant to plan, design and carry out (see Site Visit by the Strategic Leadership Advisor in Chapter Five).

Participants are expected to make all logistical arrangements for the planned SLA site visit well in advance of Day 30. This may include obtaining office space, selecting and inviting followers to attend a one-hour feedback session focusing on participant leadership skills and abilities, and a final debriefing session with the SLA.

The second session today is "needs-based" and tailored to meet the leadership information requests of each participant. Reviews of past leadership sessions, models, tools and/or concepts may be covered, depending on participant interests.

Checklists for the final full week of course activities are provided and a reminder that all reading assignments are to be completed no later than Day 30.

"Leadership is hard to define, and good leadership even harder. But if you can get people to follow you to the ends of the earth, you are a great leader."

—Indra Nooyi
Chairperson and CEO, PepsiCo

QUICK LEADERSHIP GUIDE: DAY 24

KEY TASKS & ACTIVITIES

- REVIEW OF DAY 22 AND DAY 23 LESSONS LEARNED
- ACTION PLANNING
- CHECKLISTS/ASSIGNMENTS
- IMPACT PAPER
- KEEP READING
- LOGISTICS FOR SITE VISIT

READINGS

- CONTINUATION OF ALL REQUIRED READING

COMMENTS

The 24th day of instruction focuses on completion of all remaining participant coursework and the requirements needed to obtain leadership certification. In addition, there are on-the-job assignments to complete, as well as the weekly checklist of activities to track.

It's expected all required readings are completed during the week. Journaling continues as well, to record specific problems and/or concerns participants are experiencing or they anticipate facing in their new leadership positions.

A progress check on the completion of all course requirements is scheduled for the Day 26 SLA debriefing session.

> *"Any group has a sense of who it is and what it values, but this sense often remains beneath the surface. A wise leader can discern these unspoken beliefs and articulate them."*
>
> —DIANE DREHER
> *Author of "The Tao of Inner Peace"*

QUICK LEADERSHIP GUIDE: DAY 25

KEY TASKS & ACTIVITIES

- REVIEW OF DAY 22 AND DAY 23 LESSONS LEARNED
- ACTION PLANNING
- CHECKLIST/ASSIGNMENTS
- IMPACT PAPER
- KEEP READING
- LOGISTICS FOR SITE VISIT

READINGS

- CONTINUATION OF ALL REQUIRED READING

COMMENTS

The 25th day of instruction continues the focus on completion of all remaining course tasks and requirements needed to obtain certification by the participant. It's expected participants make special efforts in the waning days of the course to apply what they've learned from live instruction to actual on-the-job situations.

This also is a day for participants to ensure logistical arrangements are underway to host the SLA during the Day 30 Site Visit. Additionally, Day 25 is an opportunity to work on Action Plans and Impact Papers

As usual, journaling should be continued as well as any remaining reading.

> "The greatest leader is not necessarily the one who does the greatest things. He is the one that gets the people to do the greatest things."
>
> —RONALD REAGAN
> 40th U.S. President

QUICK LEADERSHIP GUIDE: DAY 26

KEY TASKS & ACTIVITIES

- ONLINE LIVE DEBRIEFING WITH STRATEGIC LEADERSHIP ADVISOR (SLA)/COACH/MENTOR
- CHECKLIST
- REVIEW OF HOMEWORK
- REVIEW OF READING
- PROGRESS CHECK ON CERTIFICATION PROCESS
- JOURNALING

READINGS

- CONTINUATION OF ALL REQUIRED READING

COMMENTS

The 26th day of instruction serves as the final SLA debriefing prior to the site visit on Day 30. Participants are expected to kick off this session with a five- to 10-minute review of the week's lessons learned, as taken from their journal entries. The SLA reviews homework assignments, checklists and readings. The SLA also reviews each participant's progress in completing requirements for the QLG Professional Leadership Certificate. Participants are expected to share difficulties they're experiencing that would prevent their certification.

Logistical preparations for the site visit should be completed by now and are reviewed and discussed. The site visit's purpose and expectations are clarified, as needed. It's expected all participants continue to complete any remaining reading assignments and continue their journaling to record observations and remaining leadership questions.

"Effective team leaders adjust their style to provide what the group can't provide for itself."

—KEN BLANCHARD
Coauthor of "Leadership & The One Minute Manager"

QUICK LEADERSHIP GUIDE: DAY 27

KEY TASKS & ACTIVITIES

- REVIEW OF SLA DEBRIEFING
- KEEP READING
- ACTION PLANNING
- CHECKLISTS/ASSIGNMENTS
- IMPACT PAPER
- LOGISTICS FOR SITE VISIT
- JOURNALING

READINGS

- CONTINUATION OF ALL REQUIRED READING

COMMENTS

The 27th day of instruction will afford participants the opportunity to review the results of their Day 26 SLA/Coach/Mentor debriefing sessions and continue to complete course assignments.

Today continues participant efforts to complete any remaining logistical arrangements for the Day 30 site visit. They also are expected to continue their work on this week's homework assignments and checklist items while devoting time to their Action Plans, Impact Papers and journals.

"Not all readers are leaders, but all leaders are readers."
—HARRY S. TRUMAN
33rd U.S. President

QUICK LEADERSHIP GUIDE: DAY 28

KEY TASKS & ACTIVITIES

- REVIEW OF SLA DEBRIEFING
- ACTION PLANNING

- CHECKLISTS/ASSIGNMENTS
- IMPACT PAPER
- KEEP READING
- LOGISTICS FOR SITE VISIT
- JOURNALING

READINGS

- CONTINUATION OF ALL REQUIRED READING

COMMENTS

During the 28th day of instruction, participants are expected to have completed most (if not all) of their course requirements and assignments and are preparing themselves for their final day of live course instruction on Day 29.

Participants are expected to prepare for Day 29 by reviewing their journals for remaining leadership questions or concerns since the day will be devoted primarily to review and personal feedback.

By Day 28, it's anticipated participants have drafted their Impact Papers and Action Plans and completed all logistical arrangements for the SLA site visit on Day 30. In preparation for Day 29, participants should review their journals once more to identify any remaining leadership concerns or topics that have yet to be addressed.

> *"There is no freeway to the future, no paved highway from here to there. There is only wilderness, uncertain terrain. There are no roadmaps, no signposts. So pioneering leaders rely upon a compass and a dream."*
>
> —JAMES A. KOUZES
> *Coauthor of "The Leadership Challenge"*

QUICK LEADERSHIP GUIDE: DAY 29

KEY TASKS & ACTIVITIES

- ONLINE LIVE REVIEW OF LEADERSHIP PRINCIPLES
- ONLINE LIVE PARTICIPANT FEEDBACK
- ONLINE LIVE RECOMMENDATIONS FOR FUTURE LEADER-SHIP DEVELOPMENT ACTIVITIES
- JOURNALING

READINGS

- COMPLETION OF ALL REQUIRED READING

COMMENTS

The 29th day of the course also is the final day of online, live leadership instruction. This session, much like the second session of Day 23, will be "needs-based" and tailored to meet the specific requests of each participant. Reviews and/or clarifications of past leadership sessions, models, tools and/or concepts may be covered based on participant concerns and interests.

Participants also may use both sessions today to obtain feedback on their performance throughout the course with their QLG instructor. They may forward draft copies of Action Plans and/or Impact Papers to him/her for feedback as well. Final versions of both documents are to be submitted to the SLA on or before Day 30.

Finally, a review of all logistical arrangements for the SLA site visit is conducted, and the QLG instructor forwards any last minute changes directly to the SLA before his/her departure.

> *"A leader takes people where they want to go. A great leader takes people where they don't necessarily want to go, but ought to be."*
>
> —ROSALYN CARTER
> *Former First Lady of the U.S.*

QUICK LEADERSHIP GUIDE: DAY 30

KEY TASKS & ACTIVITIES

- SLA SITE VISIT
- SUBMISSION OF IMPACT PAPER
- SUBMISSION OF ACTION PLAN
- OBSERVATION OF LEADERSHIP ACTIVITY
- CONFIDENTIAL FOLLOWER FEEDBACK SESSION
- PARTICIPANT FEEDBACK SESSION
- COMPLETION OF CERTIFICATION PROCESS
- RECOMMENDATIONS FOR FUTURE LEADERSHIP DEVELOPMENT
- COURSE EVALUATION

READINGS

- NONE

COMMENTS

The 30th and final day of the course is the Site Visit conducted by the Strategic Leadership Advisor (SLA). The SLA begins by reviewing the day's activities while participants share and submit all course documents, completed logistical arrangements, and schedules of planned events. Key activities include the observation of a participant-led follower activity; the conducting of a confidential feedback session with followers by the SLA; a personal feedback session with the participant; and a final evaluation.

The purpose of the confidential feedback session with followers is to ascertain how the participant has been viewed and perceived over the past 30 days. The SLA expects to ask the group to provide specific suggestions for improving the participant's leadership capabilities and skills.

A personal feedback session with the participant will communicate follower feedback and provide direct performance feedback based on interactions with the SLA and other QLG faculty members throughout the course. This session will also review the various QLG Professional Leadership criteria (see Chapter 5, Site Visit by the Strategic Leadership Advisor).

If not previously submitted and evaluated, the SLA reviews final Impact Papers and Action Plans before making a final determination about successful completion of the certification process.

Participants also are asked to review their journals a final time starting with Day 1, and identify key leadership lessons learned throughout the course. Finally, participants are asked to complete a written course evaluation.

> *"I think it is important for people who are given leadership roles to assume that role immediately."*
>
> —Bob Iger
> *Chairman and CEO, The Walt Disney Company*

REFERENCES

Harden, Jim and Dude, Brad. *What Makes You Tick and What Ticks You Off: How the Basic Elements of Temperament Will Lead You to a Happier Life*. Annapolis, Maryland: Shadow Stone Publishing, 2009.

Blanchard, Kenneth H., Zigarmi, Patricia and Zigarmi, Drea. *Leadership and the One Minute Manager: Increasing Effectiveness through Situational Leadership*. New York: Morrow, 1985. Print.

Kouzes, James and Posner, Barry. *The Leadership Challenge: How to Make Extraordinary Things Happen in Organizations*, 5th Edition. A Wiley Brand, 2012.

Tuckman, Bruce (Spring 2001) "Developmental Sequence in Small Groups" (PDF). *Group Facilitation: A Research and Applications Journal*, 71-72.

Goleman, Daniel, *Leadership: The Power of Emotional Intelligence—Selected Writings*, 2011, More Than Sound.

Cloke, Kenneth, and Goldsmith, Joan. *Resolving Conflicts At Work: Ten Strategies for Everyone On The Job*. San Francisco: Jossey-Bass, 2011. Print.

Greenleaf, Robert K., *Servant Leadership: A Journey into the Nature of Legitimate Power & Greatness*. Paulist Press. The Robert K. Greenleaf Center, Inc. 2002.

All quotes are taken with permission from: AZquotes.com

De Grosbois, Teresa with Rowe, Karen. *Mass Influence: The Habits of the Highly Influential.* Copyright © Wildlife Workshops Inc., 2015.

All photos are reprinted with the approval of the photographer.

THANK YOU!

I hope you've enjoyed this, the fourth book in the *Secrets of Temperament* series, and that you're now armed with more answers about how you can become an effective leader in just 30 days!

With the quick links below, you'll be able to rate this book, Tweet, and brag about it on Facebook. Please take a moment to do that. I'd be grateful, and it will help others who are seeking to rapidly ready themselves for a leadership position.

I'd also appreciate it very much if you could leave a short review of the book on Amazon via the link below. It will help me improve this and future books, and it helps other readers like you decide if the *Secrets of Temperament* series books are right for them.

Many thanks!
Brad

Tap here to go to my Amazon Author page and rate/review this book: http://amazon.com/author/braddude

Check out all the books in the Secrets of Temperament series

Tweet about this book

Post to Facebook

Check out Brad's website at: https://braddude.com

Visit our newest website at: https://quickleadershipgroup.com

READ MORE
ABOUT IT!

I. "WHAT MAKES YOU TICK AND WHAT TICKS YOU OFF: HOW THE BASIC ELEMENTS® OF TEMPERAMENT WILL LEAD YOU TO A HAPPIER LIFE" (Jim Harden, coauthor)

This is the primary volume on the study of temperament and makes a great prerequisite for the readers of both new book series. Each of the four basic elements are described in detail and explained via stories that highlight the dominant and shadow temperaments. A forward by Ken and Scott Blanchard, noted business authors, provides unique insight into how temperament can aid in enhancing relationships and reducing conflicts at home and on the job. (AVAILABLE NOW ON AMAZON: www.amazon.com/author/braddude)

II. SECRETS OF TEMPERAMENT™ SERIES

This series of non-fiction books describes how temperament is an important factor in how one behaves often without realizing it. Each book reveals how temperament influences such routine activities as picking out a movie; driving a car; celebrating a holiday; leading an organization; and, even interacting with the people we love.

BOOK #1: *Successfully Applying the Basic Elements of Temperament: At Work!* (Jim Harden, coauthor)

This book shares insights and practical strategies for using temperament to enhance the reader's relationships while reducing conflicts with coworkers, supervisors, colleagues and executives. (AVAILABLE NOW ON AMAZON)

BOOK #2: *40 Tips for Figuring Out Your Boss!*

This book provides a practical look at how people work and communicate with *difficult* bosses. Specific tips for enhancing the personal relationship between the reader and her boss are offered based on whether she's working for an Earth, Air, Fire or Water. (AVAILABLE NOW ON AMAZON)

BOOK #3: *Keeping Our Teens Safe on the Road Should Be No Accident!* This book (with a Parental Checklist included) provides parents with specific and practical steps for aiding new family drivers in becoming safer on the streets while recognizing how temperament influences their personal reactions, attitudes towards other drivers and physical driving practices. (AVAILABLE NOW ON AMAZON)

BOOK #4: *Quick! I Need to Be a Leader in 30 Days!*

This book provides guidance to newly promoted individuals who are assuming leadership positions but have little or no leadership experience. It provides specific content for each day of instruction and includes checklists, discussion topics, recommended readings, and comments on self-study practices that can help the new leader hit the ground running in his/her new job. (AVAILABLE NOW ON AMAZON)

BOOK #5: *Successfully Applying the Basic Elements of Temperament: At Home!*

This book takes the lessons learned from understanding the basics of temperament into the home. Readers will learn how their spouses, significant others, in-laws, children, relatives and even their neighbors really perceive them! (COMING SOON)

III. TEMPERAMENT TALES™ SERIES

This series of fictional books illustrates how temperament influences the way people act and react to the behaviors of others and the emotional events that touch their lives. It places the reader in situations that typically drive them crazy and often result in surprising actions and reactions from the people they love.

BOOK #1: *The Great Shadow's Five Christmas Secrets*

This book describes how the shadow temperament often negatively influences the way people behave and how such influences can be overcome using the secrets of love, wisdom, hope and other holiday mysteries. (AVAILABLE NOW ON AMAZON)

BOOK #2: *Rubber and Glue: The Saving of a School Bully*

This book focuses on the influence of temperament on the actions of one very troubled young boy and how a brave counselor came to his aid to turn his life around. (COMING SOON)

BOOK #3: *The Great Shadow on New Year's Eve!*

This book follows the Great Shadow to a city in the middle of a swinging New Year's Eve celebration. Yet not everyone is celebrating. A riveting story reveals how your shadow temperament can change lives— surprisingly, for the better! (COMING SOON)

FOR MORE INFORMATION ABOUT LEADERSHIP

Visit my website at: https://braddude.com.

ABOUT
THE AUTHOR

Brad Dude has more than 40 years of experience as a trainer, manager and consultant to clients in more than 30 countries. He has conducted temperament and leadership seminars for such organizations as NASA, Westinghouse, the Naval Surface Warfare Center, the National Credit Union Administration, the Graduate School USA and others.

Dude consults on organization development, staff training and strategic planning with a variety of clients in the government, nonprofit and private sectors. Other clients have included: Macro International, the U.S. Agency for International Development, Reconcile/ New Orleans, the U.S. Department of Homeland Security, the U.S. Department of Energy, Louisiana Council on Aging Director's Association, Steel Authority of India, the U.S. Department of Interior, and the Peace Corps.

Dude has written extensively about temperament and how it influences the behavior of leaders, managers and employees in organizations. He is the founding director of a 30-day leadership course that complements this book. The *Quick! I Need to Be a Leader in 30 Days!* certificate course combines live online instruction with practical assignments, experiential activities and individual support and assistance.

Brad Dude lives in New Orleans with his wife Sue and has one son and three grandsons.

Explore this new leadership course at: https://quickleadershipgroup.com

Brad Dude can be contacted via LinkedIn, Twitter, and Facebook. Check out his website: https://braddude.com.